THE HISTORY OF PROSTITUTION

D0372392

THE HISTORY
OF
PROSTITUTION

GEORGE RYLEY SCOTT

SENATE

The History of Prostitution

Previously published in 1968 as *Ladies of Vice* by Tallis Press Ltd,
London

This edition published in 1996 by Senate, an imprint of
Random House UK Ltd, Random House, 20 Vauxhall Bridge
Road, London SW1V 2SA

Copyright © George Ryley Scott 1968

All rights reserved. This publication may not be reproduced,
stored in a retrieval system or transmitted, in any form or by
any means, electronic, mechanical, photocopying or otherwise,
without the prior written permission of the publishers.

ISBN 1 85958 492 6

Printed and bound in Guernsey by The Guernsey Press Co. Ltd

CONTENTS

LIST OF ILLUSTRATIONS

PART ONE

THE CAUSES OF PROSTITUTION

1: THE QUESTION OF DEFINITION

IT IS a capital error to start an examination without defining exactly what one intends to examine. It is essential, before we can deal with prostitution, that we should know exactly what a prostitute is.

Writers on the subject in the past have differed widely in their attempts at definition. Paul Lacroix in 1851 classed as prostitutes all women who were guilty of intercourse outside the married state; similarly Wardlaw, writing in 1842, defined prostitution as "the illicit intercourse of the sexes." On the other hand the popular conception of a prostitute as a woman who temporarily loans the use of her body to a miscellany of men in return for money is obviously too narrow and restricted; as is also Webster's dictionary definition, "to give up to lewdness for hire." In most cases essential factors to come within the meaning of prostitution are held to be immoral relations with at least two men contemporaneously, and for gain in each case.

It is as important to differentiate between a mistress and a prostitute as it is to differentiate between a married woman and a prostitute. The woman who lives with a man for an extended period, even though she forsakes him or is forsaken by him, and becomes the mistress of another man, is no more a prostitute, at this particular stage in her life, than a married

9

woman who obtains a divorce and marries another man is a prostitute. She may have been a prostitute before or she may become one later, but this does not affect the point. Thus to include mistresses in the category of prostitutes is to give to prostitution too wide a scope. Actually these points may not be of any great practical importance in England, but in countries where prostitutes are inscribed, the distinction is one of considerable significance.

On the other hand, to limit prostitution to those who are entirely dependent for their livelihood upon promiscuous intercourse is at once too narrow and too illogical a definition. For these constitute but a fractional part of the vast army of women who indulge in promiscuous sexual relations as a sideline or a part-time occupation, and in many instances for other reasons than those connected with pecuniary reward. The distinction between the amateur and the professional is always conceded to be a distinction of money. In its ultimate analysis it is a meaningless distinction. It overlooks the fact that one may be willing to do something, whether distasteful or not does not matter, for some form of reward or recompense other than coin of the realm. Money is merely a token. The wealthy amateur has invariably some "object" other than pure altruism. The fact that there is no cash transaction does not necessarily mean the work, in popular parlance, is done for nothing.

These amateur prostitutes, as they may be conveniently called, are increasing in all civilised countries, year by year, and, as we shall see, are continually intruding more and more upon the professional prostitute's preserves.

The contention that the disgust associated with prostitution in the mind of any respectable member of society really lies in the sex-lust which manifests itself in every transaction, and not in the mere fact that it is a trade, fails to take into account that the same argument applies to many State- and Churchauthorised marriages; just as the other contention that there can be no act of prostitution where a monetary transaction does not take place overlooks the fact that many marriages are not free from financial taint and economic considerations.

Any true definition, in contradistinction to a legal definition, of a prostitute would embrace both the professional and the amateur fornicator. The law and, in the main, the Church and the public, in their rulings, take no cognisance of anyone other than the woman who makes a living exclusively out of promiscuity. The popular supposition that the role of marriage precludes the possibility of prostitution, while in accordance with the law's interpretation, seems at variance with an ethical or a sociological viewpoint.

In indulging in promiscuous intercourse the prostitute is influenced in part or whole by some incentive other than or in addition to love or passion. The prostitute is seldom a nymphomaniac, though the nymphomaniac may become a prostitute. Nor does the absence of love from the prostitute's professional dealings imply that she is incapable of love. The twin popular assumptions that every prostitute is a volcano of lust towards all the men she can attract, and coincidentally incapable of feeling anything resembling love for any individual man, are both fallacies. It is because the prostitute, despite the fact that she may be hiring out her body to man after man without any voluptuous sensations, is capable of feeling real love for one individual man that, in some cases, is explainable the apparently inexplicable fact that it is common enough for a prostitute herself to keep what is termed a "fancy man."

Many observers contend that the absence of the love element is the one essential factor that stamps the woman as a prostitute. It is argued that a vital element in prostitution is that the woman derives no pleasure from her sexual escapades, but is concerned solely with the fees she receives in return for her services.

It seems to me, however, that the question of pleasure or otherwise cannot logically or justifiably enter into any definition of what constitutes a prostitute. Further there appears to be little in the way of actual facts to support this assumption of universal insensibility, and even the microscopic amount which does exist seems to be founded upon the most dubious premises. We all know well enough that every pleasure loses its pristine flavour if it is repeated often enough or continued long enough, and there is not the smallest doubt that prostitutes who have followed the profession for years on end can derive little or no pleasure from sexual relations to which they are so accustomed. But then it is doubtful if many married women, after regular repetitive sexual relations over a long period of years, get any pleasure from the act. The crux of the matter lies in the question of whether the prostitute, *at the commencement of her career, derives pleasure from the sex act*. And the answer, I venture to submit, is that in nine instances out of ten she does experience pleasure. She makes, in many cases, a point of combining business with pleasure, to the extent of selecting for her partners in sexual enjoyment those willing to bestow upon her money or its equivalent.

Pleasure in connection with the sex act does not necessarily imply love. Love is entirely another thing. Most men who resort to prostitutes for sexual satisfaction experience pleasure, but relatively few fall in love with the women who are mainly instrumental in providing this pleasure. The prostitute, once she is regularly embarked upon her career, rarely experiences love in the course of her work.

The female harlot, therefore, in contradistinction to the married woman (in theory, at any rate) and to the mistress, offers the use of her body to various men in exchange for money or its equivalent, and apart from or in addition to any thought of love. In many instances she goes through the sexual act and its concomitants devoid of any pleasurable feelings whatever; often, indeed, her feelings for her temporary lover are dislike or even hatred. That she performs her part in the transaction competently and apparently passionately is not, as is so often thought, evidence of her sensuality or lust; it is merely a tribute to her skill as a professional love-maker.

It is true that many married women have no feelings of love for their husbands even at the time of marriage; it is equally true that soon after marriage thousands of wives develop frigidity and *anaesthesia sexualis* towards the men they are supposed to love. In these cases the only thing that distinguishes the role of such a woman from that of a prostitute is that *one* man has contracted for the use of her body, and that the contract is sanctioned and upheld by Church and State.

There is, too, the question of the male prostitute. Prostitution is not exclusively a woman's profession; nor are those who consort with and support prostitutes members of the male sex exclusively. Male prostitutes, often euphemistically described as gigolos, are employed and paid by women; catamites are employed by homosexual and perverted men. Thus our definition of a prostitute must include both sexes, and bearing this essential point in mind, as well as our previous observations, we arrive at the following: A prostitute is an individual, female or male, who for some kind of reward, monetary or otherwise, or for some form of personal satisfaction other than purely for the gratification of an awareness of love, and as a part-time or whole-time profession, engages in normal or abnormal sexual intercourse with a number of persons, who may be of the same sex as, or the opposite sex to, herself or himself. In the succeeding pages, however, we shall deal only with female prostitution.

13

II: THE SOCIAL STANDING OF THE PROSTITUTE

TODAY many, if not most, men and women of respectability look upon the prostitute with contempt or pity, or both. Even men who are largely responsible for the profession's existence, and who affect the society of its practitioners in drinking lounges and night clubs, when in the company of female relatives or friends refrain from any discussion of prostitution, are studiously careful not to patronise any cafés which cater for women of easy virtue, and greet with icy stares the *filles de joie* with whom they have spent the previous night. The prostitute is often referred to as a "moral outcast," and, generally speaking, the reaction of polite society to her is analogous to its reaction towards an ugly family skeleton which one would like to bury decently.

So universal is this attitude that it is not unnatural there is an impression abroad that this same reaction towards the prostitute has always been current. It is a mistaken assumption. The prostitute's profession has not always been a shameful profession. On the contrary, at one time the harlot was an object of reverence and adoration, as anyone who is well acquainted with the Bible and its contemporary literature must know. In fact, at one time, in certain races, according to Lord Avebury, prostitutes were in even higher regard than were legitimately married women. In Athens they held the highest possible rank; in Vesali, too, the "chief of the courtesans" received a degree of veneration approaching that given to those of holy or chieftain blood. Even today, in Japan, and among certain primitive races, the profession of the prostitute is not one of shame.

The kedēshōth mentioned in the Bible were prostitutes attached to the Canaanite temples, and were held in the highest reverence by the worshippers. Temple prostitutes, in all countries, and at all times, have been highly thought of, and in cases where this service to their god was of a temporary nature, found no difficulty in contracting marriage. According to Strabo, among the ancient Armenians, who prostituted their daughters to the service of their god, these temporary harlots married without the slightest smudge upon their characters. Again the Babylonian women were similarly not looked down upon. On the contrary they were considered to be women who, in the true spirit of religious devotion, sacrificed their lives to the service of their god; and as such received a degree of veneration and of respect that is usually reserved for those moving in the most exalted circles.

All of which goes to show that the practice of professional prostitution under the licence of religion was viewed through a vastly different pair of spectacles from those which are turned upon it today. But I shall have more to say on this subject when I come to deal with sacred prostitution in a later stage of this inquiry.

In Japan the prostitute is not looked down upon as she is in European countries. No vulgar or derogatory terminology is used in referring to her. For instance, there is not, in the Japanese language, anything equivalent to the English whore[1]

[1] The word "whore", although widely employed in England, and particularly in early literature, is, according to the writer of the article on "Prostitution" in *The Encyclopædia Britannica* (eleventh edition), not Anglo-Saxon at all, but comes from Scandinavia, being derived from the earlier forms "hore" and "hoore." When the revised version

or harlot. The word which we translate as prostitute really signifies "temporary wife." Many of the girls attached to the *maisons de plaisir* in Japan in later years married and lived in conditions of the utmost respectability.

In India prostitutes were never looked upon as in any sense of the word degraded or immoral creatures. According to Meyer, "the Hindu has always sung the praises of 'the public woman' as the very type and embodiment of perfect womanhood."[1]

Much of this toleration of intercourse outside the married state is due to the males in many primitive races valuing neither virginity itself nor the exclusive right to sexual connection with any particular woman. In many savage tribes, as a mark of honour, a male guest is allowed by the husband or father to sleep with his wife or his daughter.

With the advent of civilisation and the patriarchal system such a thing became plainly intolerable. But, recognising that, to the majority of men, the provision of a temporary love partner constitutes a source of pleasure, in many civilised countries it became customary to provide guests of honour with high-class prostitutes or courtesans. We see evidence of this in the custom in Germany and other countries in the Middle Ages of giving visiting members of royal houses free entry into the brothels of the city. In 1434, on his visit to Ulm, King Sigismund was escorted through the gates of the city by prostitutes. In the sixteenth century, any foreign envoys visiting the Swiss town of Zürich were entertained at table not by the town officials and their wives but by the town officials and certain picked harlots from the city brothels. And although anything of this nature would not be tolerated

of the New Testament was prepared, "harlot" was substituted wherever "whore" appeared in the older version.

[1] Johann Jakob Meyer, *Sexual Life in Ancient India*, Routledge, 1930, Vol. I, p. 264.

today, there have been instances even in recent years, where, in certain foreign cities, on occasions when meetings and conferences were held, the provision of special facilities, or the extension of existing ones, for enabling visitors to come into contact with prostitutes were apparently connived at by the authorities.[1]

Coincidentally with the English concept of degradation and shame was the old notion that every prostitute was necessarily a girl of feeble mentality. Tarnowsky, a Russian authority on sex, held the view that professional prostitutes, as a result of their heredity coupled with arrested or incomplete development, were mental degenerates. Many students of the subject in the past have formed somewhat similar conclusions to that of Tarnowsky. I am of opinion, however, that there are the strongest grounds for supposing these views to have been greatly exaggerated. For the most part they were based upon the researches of social, moral and religious workers, or upon the statistics furnished in the past by Magdalen hospitals, prisons, rescue homes and the like. In consequence they were drawn from observations concerned with the lowest class of prostitute only, and they gave a quite false impression as regards prostitution as a whole. There have always been very considerable numbers of prostitutes of normal mentality and education, as anyone who has come in contact with the better class of women, and the more successful, must admit.

In every consideration of the professional prostitute one must always bear in mind the attitude of society towards this type of woman. The prostitute is a social outcast, decried, sneered at and denounced by all respectable members of society, both men and women. The men who patronise harlots and enable them to live, whatever attitude they adopt in strict

---

[1] Important business contacts in the United States are today frquently provided with "call-girls" in order to improve business relationships.

privacy, sneer at them in public. Woman's attitude towards the prostitute is slightly different from man's. In her case, it is not mere disgust or contempt; it is disgust tinctured with hatred for and jealousy of a successful rival. The married woman cannot rid herself of the idea that the prostitute is offering something outside marriage, which is, or should be, an exclusive part of the marriage contract. The single woman at one time was bothered by the idea that the street woman was to some extent spoiling her chances of getting married.

Much of the horror associated with prostitution is more a matter of terminology than of anything else. It is the word prostitute, or whore, or harlot, that has more to do with arousing feelings of disgust than the actual promiscuity connected with the trade. Even the prostitute herself, in many cases, bursts into hot rage and fiercely resents the appellation of whore. In all circumstances where promiscuity was considered respectable, it was rarely called prostitution by its practitioners. Thus the harlots attached to Moabite, Canaanite and Assyrian temples were not called prostitutes at all, but priestesses: it was the Hebrews who referred to them as whores. The *hetæræ* of ancient Greece were never referred to, or looked upon, as common harlots. And neither, down through the ages, were the French and Italian courtesans who presided over salons thronged with the intelligentsia of Europe, the mistresses of kings and aristocrats. So true is all this that today mistresses rank as respectable women.

III: THE UNDERLYING CAUSE

THE fundamental cause of female prostitution does not rest with the woman at all; it rests with the male animal. It is a biological cause. This is never stated bluntly, but it is admitted by implication.

The reasons which induce women to take up prostitution as a career are confused with the basic cause of prostitution itself, which is something quite different. In its essence prostitution is physical. Its existence is due to the physiological urge which drives the virile male animal to search for his mate and to have intercourse with her. It is, stated in plain language, the self-same urge as that which actuates the dog hanging around the bitch which is on heat.

It is this biological urge which has led, during the two thousand years of the Christian era, a sizable army of religious, moral and social leaders to look upon prostitution as an evil which must be endured; a cancerous sore which can never be eradicated but can only be checked. Always at the back of their minds was the fear that the eradication of prostitution, supposing it were possible, would bring worse evils in its train. It is this viewpoint which causes governments to view with tolerant eyes the "camp followers" of the soldiers during peace and war, and even on occasion to go so far as to provide brothels for the use of troops stationed in foreign lands.

All through the ages prostitution has presented a knotty problem; and nothing in all the world has provided a more pronounced subject for the hypocrisy of the theologians and the self-elected guardians of public morals. The difficulty they have always been faced with, and which they are faced with today, is to justify the denunciation of something which they consider it would be inadvisable to suppress; and, in addition, to justify the punishment and ostracism of one party only to a contract (which is conceded to be evil) between two parties. For prostitution exists not because it is impossible to suppress it in the sense that murder, or robbery, or infanticide, is suppressed; but because no really thorough or sincere attempt has ever been made at suppression. In some countries it is openly regulated; in others it is curbed, restricted, and, to some extent, curtailed; in none is it rigidly suppressed.

This attitude of coincident denunciation of something against which only half-hearted measures of regulation or restriction have been taken has required a certain amount of justification. The plea for toleration of the evil has always taken, despite modern ornamentation, the fundamental lines laid down by Saint Augustine seventeen hundred years ago. He held that the prostitute was an essential member of society. Sinful she was, depraved she was, sordid she was; but she was required for the express purpose of keeping lust within bounds and in proper channels. Just as Saint Paul before him had contended that although all sexual intercourse was sinful, yet it were better to marry than to "burn"; so Saint Augustine contended that despite the immorality of all fornication it were better that man should sin with a prostitute for his partner than that he should rape a respectable woman. In his own words: "What is more base, empty of worth and full of vileness than harlots and other such pests? Take away harlots from human society and you will have tainted everything with lust. Let them be with the matrons and you will produce contamination and disgrace. So this class of persons, on account of their morals, of a most shameless life, fills a most vile function under the laws of order." Similarly, according to Athenæus, Solon sanctioned the purchase of female slaves to be used as prostitutes in order to prevent the raping of respectable women; and Salvianus stated that the Romans established brothels as a preventive of adultery.

On the whole, however, theologians after Saint Augustine's day contented themselves with wholesale and comprehensive denunciation of all intercourse outside the married state, and where it became necessary to give any explicit opinion, with a denouncement of prostitution generally. Sexual intercourse itself ceased to be a subject for theological denunciation; and with the sanctifying of marriage the views of Saint Paul and his contemporaries were judiciously ignored, glossed over, or converted into a specific injunction against intercourse outside the marital state. Fornication became the special purlieu of prostitution and was condemned unreservedly.

So matters rested until in the early part of the eighteenth century Mandeville, in his notorious satire *The Fable of the Bees,* re-stated the doctrine of Saint Augustine, propounding the theory that society was indebted to the prostitute for the safety of female morals. A century later others took up the tale. Schopenhauer averred that prostitutes were "human sacrifices on the altar of monogamy"; Lecky justified the harlot's existence on the grounds that she was "the most efficient guardian of virtue"; Balzac, writing of prostitutes in his *Physiology of Marriage,* said "they sacrifice themselves for the republic and make of their bodies a rampart for the protection of respectable families." And others hymned the same tune. Man's sexual needs outside marriage, and his polygamous nature, both of which were admitted by implication if not explicitly, and woman's coincidental need of protection against man, were the justifications for prostitution which have continued to hold sway wherever and whenever the problem has received consideration.

With all this granted, it seems strange that, at the same time, the true cause of prostitution, and the fact that man is mainly responsible for its existence, have not been realised and admitted. It seems strange that, after these admissions, students of the subject should present as the major cause of prostitution the economic need of woman. True, this is a contributory cause (as I shall attempt to show in the next chapter), but it is not the basic cause. The need for woman to earn a living outside orthodox respectable forms of labour, and of marriage, does not mean, as is so often submitted, that prostitution must exist. The real cause is the sexual appetite of man. This appetite creates the demand for fornication outside the married state; and the fact that man is willing to pay for the means of satisfying his sexual requirements brings into being the professional prostitute. Were man unable or unwilling to pay the price asked there would be no professional prostitutes, but there would be an enormous increase in the number of cases of rape and seduction. Thus Saint Augustine's original dictum, supplemented by Lecky, Schopenhauer, Balzac *et alia* is dependent upon man being able to pay for his pleasure. The alternative to rape and seduction, in circumstances where economic conditions precluded the payment of the prostitute by her clients, would be the provision of free professional public women by the State either as slaves or paid fornicators.

Man is essentially polygamous, and the development of civilisation extends this innate polygamy. In any society, therefore, where comparatively a small proportion only can afford polygamy, or a succession of wives (which is really polygamy legalised and camouflaged), or a number of mistresses, the majority of men must have recourse to prostitutes, professional or amateur.

Every step forward in civilisation extends man's biological

urge for fornication, where it does not express itself along homosexual or perverted lines. Sexual stimulation develops alongside civilisation. It is a fact that domesticated animals have sexual appetites developed far in advance of animals in the wild state. Every zoologist knows the truth of this. It is a fact that the two primary things with which mankind is concerned, as Marx pointed out, are food and sex. In a race where the struggle for existence is a difficult one, food dominates sex; in civilisation, where the struggle for food, as regards a big proportion of the people, is no longer anything to worry about, sex dominates food. The tendency in modern luxurious life, where every decade the standard of living becomes higher, is towards a sex-dominated age, as in England and America today. In such circumstances, where men and women are more and more brought into intimate and disturbing contacts, where sex-appeal is a cultivated feminine art, continence becomes increasingly more difficult. The evil effects of continence are not due to continence in itself, but to the forcing of continence upon a sexually stimulated nation.

IV: REASONS WHICH LEAD WOMEN
TO BECOME PROSTITUTES

IT WAS a popular assumption, based upon the statements of
Salvation Army officials, secretaries of societies for reclaiming
"fallen women", and so forth, that prostitutes were driven into
their life of shame through sheer inability to secure work of a
respectable nature.

The reasons for the persistence of this assumption for so
long are many. For one thing, later writers of tracts on prostitution were misled by old and obsolete authorities, such, for
instance, as Parent-Duchâtelet, who said "lack of work and
insufficient wages are the main causes of prostitution"; by
Sanger, who considered that practically all prostitutes are the
"poor victims of circumstances," and would reform if they
were given the chance; and by Sherwell, who speaking specifically of prostitution in England, said "morals fluctuate with
trade."

Now the conditions which applied a hundred years ago do
not apply today. At that time practically the only respectable
occupation open to women was marriage. The alternative was
domestic service, a form of work which in those days at any
rate carried with it a degree of social obloquy or was not far
removed from slavery. Thus, for the thousands of women of
the working-classes who were not lucky enough to get married,
the only alternative to domestic service, as regards the huge

majority, was to go on the streets. The reports of servant girls who had been seduced and found it impossible to secure re-engagements in many cases formed the basis of these stories of girls driven to a life of shame to avoid starvation. But even so, it would appear that, from their own researches, these old writers missed the true significance of the enormous proportion of street walkers who had come from the ranks of domestic servants.[1] Not all of these, by any means, could possibly have been seduced, or have lost their situations through causes which prevented re-engagement. It should have been obvious that a considerable proportion deliberately left service to become ladies of joy, or to use the quaint Victorian expression, to become "gay".[2]

But however debatable this point may be as regards the past, today it admits of no debate whatever. No girl is driven into a life of prostitution through inability to secure a job. Nor will the contention that through some slight moral lapse a girl is unable to secure further work hold water any longer. Through the change in the attitude towards moral peccadilloes, the mother of an illegitimate child is no longer shunned, and indeed, of course, through more widespread contraceptive

---

[1] Sanger found that out of 2,000 New York prostitutes, 933 had formerly been in domestic service. Other writers similarly affirmed that the vast majority of prostitutes were recruited from the servant class. Merrick, during his chaplainship of Millbank Prison, found that no less than 53 per cent. of the prostitutes he had to deal with had been servants; while Sherwell stated that the Salvation Army's register showed that 88 per cent. started life in service. More recently (1916) the anonymous authors of *Downward Paths* gives domestic service as the previous occupation of 293 out of 830 prostitutes, and state: "The overwhelming preponderance of domestic servants is in agreement with all other statistics that we have seen."

[2] Very interesting light is thrown on the whole subject of the economics of Victorian prostitution by the Drs Eberhard and Phyllis Kronhausen in their presentation of *Walter, My Secret Life* (Polybooks, 2 volumes, 9/6d each.)

knowledge and facilities there was for a long time a noticeable decline in the number of pregnancies outside marriage.

All of which does not mean that the underlying cause is not economic. It is. It is economic in the sense that dissatisfaction with their position leads most girls to embark upon the career of the prostitute. Shop-girls, factory workers, in fact all employees in the lower-paid and more servile walks of life, are eager to grasp any opportunity to get away from their environment.

Poverty is not a matter than can be defined ecumenically. What to one person is poverty, to another is comparative wealth. Nor can it be measured solely in terms of money. There are conditions of employment which, to some girls, are not nearly so endurable as prostitution. There are conditions of marriage which involve mental cruelty and degradation such as the successful harlot may never know.

As regards 95 per cent. of the prostitutes in this or any other civilised country, the profession is deliberately chosen. It may be, and it is, chosen for a variety of reasons, and often through the influence of environmental factors, but it is chosen in preference to other forms of occupation which are available. So that, in strict truth, as regards the huge majority, what it is customary to call *causes* of prostitution are rather *reasons* for the taking up of the profession of prostitute.

These reasons are many. One cannot point a finger at any particular one and say this is the sole reason. One cannot fix upon a certain social failing which should be remedied or a certain reform which should be instituted, and say this is the solution of the whole difficulty.

Generally speaking, however, the main reasons which induce girls to take up prostitution are love of luxury and idleness. Often the two are combined.[1]

[1] It is interesting to note that the report of the Committee on

The one breeds the other to such an extent that it becomes difficult to separate them. In ever-increasing numbers girls are willing to buy their way to ease, position and fame through the sale of their bodies. Certain shop-girls, typists, chorus girls, factory workers and a host of others working at plebeian jobs, who possess any pretence to prettiness, and who, besides having few scruples, are not averse to indulging in amorous adventure, do not experience the smallest difficulty in finding men who are willing to take them out and to buy them luxuries in exchange for their sexual favours.

For to tell the truth, in many cases, they place, these girls, few obstacles in the path. They are usually delighted to have the opportunity to be taken out to dinner, to a theatre, and to have a good time generally. Some show girls of a *blasé* type are notorious for their free and easy morals, and many of them are indistinguishable from professional prostitutes in all but name. Probably most stage-struck girls, in any case, believe that they must make themselves sexually available to get any chance at all of climbing towards the stardom which they so feverishly seek.

The first step having been taken, the rest is easy. The girl becomes what is best described as an amateur prostitute. It is easy to see how from this she can gradually drift into full-time prostitution. The life is comparatively easy, there is no drudgery of work attached to it, and in its initial stages, at any rate, once the step has been taken, it is not without its glamour. There is, further, no disputing the fact that the higher-class prostitute often comes into contact with men in a far better social position than she could ever have hoped to meet had

Homosexual Offences and Prostitution published in London in 1957 stated: "Our impression is that the great majority of prostitutes are women whose psychological make-up is such that they choose this life because they find in it a style of living which is to them easier, freer and more profitable than would be provided by any other occupation."

she continued in the walk of life in which God or circumstance had placed her.

It is all very well for the woman moving in expensive circles, whose parents are wealthy, or who is married to a well-to-do husband, to express amazement at any girl choosing so degrading a profession as that of a harlot. It is all very well for the raddled and dour Puritan, who is so ugly or so unattractive that the most gorgeous upholstery would only serve to intensify rather than to camouflage her shortcomings, to express similar amazement. But neither the one nor the other knows anything about the reasons which induce the girl of poor parentage to look with envy on the successful *fille de joie*. Born of parents and in an environment which hold out less than the faintest hope of anything beyond a job in a factory or as a shop assistant, with the ultimate hope of marrying an uninspiring and unambitious working man of her own station and *milieu*, with a drab future to look forward to, it is not surprising that many such girls seek escape in prostitution from the prospect of the tyranny of household monotony.

This view has always been prevalent. The children in poor quarters of big cities are often brought up in circumstances where there is no mystery attached to the sexual parts or even to the sexual act itself. Promiscuity is thought little of. The overcrowding which, even in these civilised days as well as for decades past, is rife in every town, causes whole families to sleep in one bedroom. Brothers take liberties with their sisters; mutual masturbation is common; incestuous relations are often the inevitable aftermath.[1] And in the country villages conditions are sometimes hardly any better. The sexual sophistication of country-bred youngsters who are familiar with the genetics of animals often far exceeds that of their

[1] The author of *The Prevention of Destitution* (London, 1912) said that among the slum children "to have a baby by your father is laughed at as a comic mishap."

28

contemporaries who live in the cities. Little wonder that girls reared in such circumstances commit sexual misconduct at an early age, and often drift to a life of prostitution as a matter of course. Moreover, in such an atmosphere, there is inculcated neither respect nor admiration for marriage. On the contrary, the sight of quarrels, of drudgery, of marital boorishness is only too likely to make children look upon prostitution as infinitely preferable to marriage.

In their own primitive way these girls of the poorest quarters have grasped the fact which Marro (quoted by Ellis) observes: "The actual conditions of society are opposed to any high moral feeling in women, for between those who sell themselves to prostitution and those who sell themselves to marriage the only difference is in price and duration of the contract." Both in marriage and in prostitution, sex is the bait which woman offers to man. Sex represents the basis of her bargaining. In the case of marriage she holds out for a lifelong partnership or its economic equivalent; in the case of prostitution she accepts a price varying according to circumstances and in all cases representing the best bargain she is able to make for a temporary sexual association.

There are circumstances, too, in which even women of good family will choose prostitution as a profession. They may, through conditions over which they have no control whatever, be compelled to choose between prostitution and suicide or death from starvation. The histories of nations that have gone through the throes of revolution or have suffered invasion by enemy forces provide instances of many starving and destitute refugees having to make just this choice. They were on foreign soil, they knew nothing of the language, they were neither trained nor fitted for work of any kind. Naturally inevitably, in sheer despair, they elected to sell that which finds a ready market wherever men forgather.

Much conflict of opinion exists as to how far sex itself enters into the choice of the profession of prostitute. Morasso says that sexual desire constitutes the main causative factor, and would have us believe that the majority of prostitutes are nymphomaniacs or something not very far removed from that. At the other extreme is Lombroso, who asserts that prostitutes are frigid; and Maverick, writing in specific reference to London prostitutes, backs up Lombroso's assertion. On the whole, the majority of investigators incline to the view that sensuality is often a predisposing factor in the choice of prostitution as a profession; and this, too, is the view held by the public, strengthened by the evidence of men who have associated with professional harlots.

In very many cases, however, a simulated sensuality or show of passion may well be mistaken for the real thing. It should never be forgotten that sex is the prostitute's trade; that she has all the tricks of this trade at her finger tips. The simulation of passion and, more still, of lust as a means of exciting the sexual passion of her partner by gratifying his needs or requirements in ways from which a woman of respectability would shrink even if she had any knowledge of their technique, and sometimes to the extent of indulging in perverse practices, have again had a lot to do with the reputation for gross sensuality which the professional harlot has earned for herself. The client of the prostitute, himself gorged with lust, somewhat naturally credits his partner with similar feelings to his own.

It is doubtful, therefore, whether prostitutes, *in the main,* at the time of selecting their career, are more sexual than are their respectable sisters. It is, of course, exceedingly difficult to secure any worthwhile evidence on this point. It is futile to ask the prostitutes themselves.

It is equally doubtful whether they are more frigid than are females in any other class of society. Statements upon which any observations respecting the frigidity of prostitutes are based have been almost wholly drawn from *old harlots,* and because of this, if for no other reason, are of little value. For while there may conceivably be some room for doubt as to the sensuality or lack of it in young and successful practitioners, in the case of the old and unsuccessful ones there is little room for doubt. The old harlot is invariably frigid. She tends to become more and more frigid as she plies her profession. There is abundant evidence of this in the universality of masturbation among prostitutes and in the commonness of homosexuality. The woman who derives pleasure from normal intercourse seldom masturbates, and even more seldom is she addicted to homosexuality. It is the lack of pleasure associated with coitus which on the one hand induces and develops masturbatory practices as a means of satisfying sexual desire; and which on the other hand turns her against intercourse with the opposite sex outside her work, and often leads to the development of homosexual tendencies. The argument that she may have been a homosexual before she became a prostitute will not hold water. It is rare to a degree for a homosexual woman to take up professional prostitution apart from tribadism. But, on the contrary, prostitution is a potent factor in the development of homosexuality and in the fostering of perverse practices. In this connection Moll's assertion that lesbianism was common among Berlin prostitutes—no less than 25 per cent. of them being addicted to its practice— is worthy of note.

If nymphomania were more general it would be a predisposing cause of prostitution of some significance. But nymphomania, though admittedly much more common than in previous ages, is not general enough to affect more than a small proportion of those who become professional harlots.

At one time it did most assuredly lead a woman to become a prostitute. In ancient Rome there were ladies of gentle birth who became registered as public prostitutes in order to obtain satisfaction for their sexual passions and appetites. Others had slaves for the express purpose of providing them with sexual pleasure. But in these days of female emancipation a nymphomaniac has opportunities for indulging, under the guise of respectability, in her passion for venery that were unavailable to women of other generations. The modern girl who is allowed to go for unchaperoned car rides, week-end jaunts and holidays, with a succession of young men, is in an entirely different position from that of the guarded maiden of pre-1914.

The force of example is a factor not to be overlooked, especially in these days when parents more and more exhibit a tendency to allow their daughters to leave home and live in rooms. Undoubtedly it leads to a certain number of such girls taking up prostitution as a part-time or whole-time profession. A girl happens to secure lodgings in the same building as an amateur prostitute and makes her acquaintance; or, quite unknowingly, she is led to share a room or a flat with one. The sequel, often enough, is that in a relatively short time there are two amateur prostitutes where before there was only one.

Undoubtedly, too, the sharing of apartments or rooms is not without its dangers. It *may possibly* lead to a form of promiscuity which is usually ignored or overlooked in any consideration of prostitution, to wit, female homosexuality or lesbianism. It is quite impossible to make any kind of estimate respecting the extent of female homosexuality in this or any other country. The practice of girls living together is so common that it is rare for the possibility of anything evil resulting from it to be in any way associated with it. And there are no references, veiled or unveiled, in reports of police court cases, to lesbianism, which, even to the extent of indulgence in overt practices, is not a criminal offence. While, it is true, most of these homosexual alliances are foolish rather than harmful, going little beyond kissing and cuddling, there is always the risk of degeneration into perversity, especially where the professional element enters into it. Where true tribadism is concerned, perverse practices are common, ranging from mutual masturbation and *cunnilinctus* to the use of some mechanical device, referred to variously as *godemiché*, dildo, *consolateur*, *bijou indiscret*, baubo and *penis succedaneus*, which would appear to have been employed by savage as well as civilised races in all parts of the world. Among the earliest references to its use are those in the *Mimes of Herodas*, in the *Lysistrata* of Aristophanes and in the Bible.

V: REASONS WHY MEN SUPPORT
PROSTITUTION

THE men who have recourse to prostitutes to satisfy their
sexual appetites are both single and married, young and old.

It may be taken as axiomatic that the average man patron-
ises prostitutes through sheer necessity only. In other words,
he seeks solace with a prostitute when no other woman, capable
or willing to satisfy his wants, is available. With exceptions
so few as to be negligible, men are well aware of all the
disadvantages and risks attendant on intercourse with ladies
of vice. In fact, the tendency, if anything, is for these risks
to be exaggerated.

In the first place, nine men out of ten dread contracting a
venereal infection; in the second place, to the huge majority,
the patronage of a prostitute represents an extravagance
which can be indulged in at intervals only; in the third place,
many men, after spending a time with a harlot, feel a certain
amount of disgust with themselves and are not at all anxious
that their escapade should become public knowledge. For all
these reasons in general, and occasionally for some other
additional reason in particular, it may be taken for granted
that the prostitute is the last resource.

We have seen that the basic underlying cause of prostitution is the biological fact that man calls for sexual intercourse
almost as universally and as regularly as he calls for food and

the other necessaries of life. Admitting the male appetite for sexual intercourse, modern observers and moralists contend that if man could be induced to marry at an earlier age the death-knell of prostitution would be sounded; that if man could be provided with the safe, legal and inexpensive means of satisfying the demands of his sexual appetite, which means marriage provides, he would cease to patronise the prostitute.

Marriage and prostitution are inextricably interlinked. Every bond which makes the monogamous marriage system more secure coincidentally extends promiscuity in the form of prostitution, free love or adultery. It is the realisation of all this that has led the clergy and the moralists either to lament the necessity for prostitution or to wink at its indulgence. The ancients and the early Christians realised the impossibility of having one without the other. Thus the efforts of Saint Augustine, of Cato and of Aquinas to justify it, to which reference has already been made. In more recent years Liguori and others have expressed similar views. So, too, the philosophers and thinkers. These views then, expressed or unexpressed, may be taken to be behind the male attitude towards prostitution, rammed home by the fact that the male justifies his need of sex experience by expressing the view, whether he believes it or not, that coitus is essential to every man as a means of preserving his health. It is the biological justification of his support of the prostitute.

These arguments are based upon an inadequate knowledge of sex and its problems. Their falsity is amply demonstrated by the fact that married men as well as single men patronise prostitutes. Indeed, there are firm grounds for the assumption that married men provide, if not the majority, certainly the more remunerative section, of the harlot's clientele.

The motive which drives a man into the arms of a prostitute in preference or in addition to those of his wife may be any one of a dozen conceivable reasons. In the first place there are the preponderating number of men, especially single men unversed in the mysteries of sex, and married men whose sexual adventures are limited to the women they have married, whose sexual appetites, once they have been thoroughly aroused, cannot be satiated by any one respectable woman, and who subscribe too literally to the doctrine, propounded with Rabelaisian humour by Benjamin Franklin, that all women are alike in the dark. In a document,[1] which is in the form of a letter addressed "To My Dear Friend," the famous American author, statesman and inventor wrote: "I know of no medicine fit to diminish the violent natural inclinations you mention; and if I did, I think I should not communicate it to you. Marriage is the proper remedy. It is the most natural state of man, and therefore the state in which you are most likely to find solid happiness. Your reasons against entering into it at present appear to me not well founded." After a short disquisition on the benefits of the marital state, he observed: "But if you will not take this counsel and persist in thinking a commerce with the sex inevitable, then in all your amours you should prefer old women to young ones." Franklin then goes on to present a number of reasons for this

[1] This letter, which was written in 1745 to some correspondent whose name, if known, has never been disclosed, and was probably intended for reading to a select circle of cronies, much as Robert Burns was accustomed to read his collection of salacious verse, was discovered years after Franklin's death in an accumulation of documents and correspondence. It was eventually purchased, along with many other manuscripts, by the United States Government. This particular document, known as *A Letter to a Young Man on the Choice of a Mistress*, the existence of which had long been known to a few, was rigidly suppressed until comparatively recently, and gained for itself a notoriety equal to that associated with the satirical Franklin document entitled *A Letter on Perfumes to the Academy of Brussels*.

There is an excellent anthology of Burns's bawdy poems and a first-class life of the Bard published by Luxor Press at 9/6d, under the title: *The Merry Muses and other Burnsian Frolics*.

advice. Among these reasons are: the increased knowledge of the world that comes with age; the fact that "when women cease to be handsome they study to be good"; their continued amiability in advancing years; the solicitation and tenderness they display in times of sickness; the absence of any risk of conception; and their greater prudence and discretion "in conducting an intrigue." This catalogue of advantages peculiar to the aged female does not end here. The author continues: "Because in every animal that walks upright the deficiency of the fluids that fill the muscles appears first in the highest part. The face first grows lank and wrinkled, then the neck, then the breast and arms, . . . so that covering all above with a basket, and regarding only what is below the girdle, it is impossible of two women to know an old one from a young one. And as in the dark all cats are grey, the pleasure of corporal enjoyment with an old woman is at least equal, and frequently superior; every knack being by practice capable of improvement." Other reasons given are "the sin is less," likewise the "compunction." Presumably a subscriber to Saint Paul's celebrated dictum, Benjamin Franklin concludes: "But still I advise you to marry directly."

Now, like most of the facile aphorisms expressed by sophisticated rodomontadists, amateur Casanovas, smart-alecks and merchants of bravura, the notion that all women are alike in respect of their capacity for giving sexual satisfaction to men is a fallacy. The error is due to the cynical vaporisings of those who are blind to the psychological factors affecting sexual intercourse on the one hand, and the great variations in the technique of coitus and its connotations on the other. Where the pleasure connected with sex is a purely physical pleasure, coitus is, at best, a poor affair, and is little removed from a masturbatory process. It is in such a case that the personality and appearance of the woman count for nothing— the man is oblivious to female charm and individuality. His attitude towards marriage is wholly wrong. He considers its main object to be the provision of opportunities for unrestrained sexual indulgence.

Most men, however, of any intelligence or culture find that the charm, beauty and personality of the woman produce physical and psychological repercussions which in turn have considerable effect upon the satisfaction and pleasure resulting from sexual intercourse itself. Also there are numerous women to whom the sexual side of married life is a matter of indifference; there are others to whom it is repellent. This discovery is sometimes not made by the male partner until after marriage, and often enough it comes as a most disturbing and disappointing revelation. The result, in a case where the husband possesses any delicacy of feeling or sensitivity, is that he in turn, in consequence of frustration, develops indifference and his love for his wife wanes.

The prostitute, in a very large number of cases, can arouse a man's sexual passion where his wife completely fails. It is not alone the allure of a strange woman, which invariably possesses some power as an aphrodisiac; but partly it is due to the mastery of the knack of arousing sensual thoughts that the harlot undoubtedly possesses. Her mode of dress, her manner, her conversation: all are deliberately designed to one end. The result is that mere proximity to a prostitute will often arouse in a married man a degree of sexual desire that, after the honeymoon weeks, he rarely experiences when in the company of his wife.

It is due to all these reasons that there are married men, and they are not few in number, who, while they have the highest degree of reverence and respect for their wives, are yet so little aroused sexually in their presence that they seldom experience the slightest desire for sexual intercourse with them; yet in the company of other women these same men are goaded almost beyond endurance. Men of this type, who are married to women of charm, culture and beauty, and yet regularly consort with prostitutes, are a puzzle to their friends and acquaintances unversed in the problems and subtleties of sexual psychology.

Then again, it must be remembered that beauty is not of the faintest value as an indication of sexual appetite or capacity. There are women rivalling the most beautiful film stars in appearance who prove to have no more sexual passion than a eunuch. The men they marry usually find this out only after marriage.

Old men are frequent clients of prostitutes. In addition to the fact that all ordinary methods of arousing sexual passion have long since ceased to produce the slightest effect, and only abnormal methods of stimulation will induce the desired results, most sensual old men have a penchant for young and pretty females. Their wives no longer possess the faintest attraction for them sexually.

There is, too, a widespread belief in the revitalising and rejuvenating power which coitus with a young girl, and especially a virgin, possesses for an old man. It is based upon the theory that some vital fluid is absorbed during the act of intercourse. Students of the Bible will recall that David performed the sexual act with the young Abishag for this very purpose.

Finally, there are the sexual perverts, old and young, married and single, who are regular clients of prostitutes. They constitute, these perverts, a far larger proportion of men than most people have any conception of. There are in particular the fetishists, who can only perform the sexual act in certain circumstances or in special surroundings. There were in former days brothels in Paris and other Continental cities where such men were accommodated. Tarnowsky quotes the extreme case mentioned in Taxil's *La Prostitution contemporaine*, where a special apartment in a Parisian brothel was draped in black satin, with silver ornamentation, and a prostitute, laid full length upon a bed, her face and body whitened, played the role of a corpse for the benefit of necrophiles. These and other elaborate arrangements for satisfying the whims of wealthy patrons were features of the more expensive houses of prostitution.

Men who, through age, long-continued depravity or other causes, are temporarily or permanently stricken with impotence, in the brothels found companions who would allow them to wear mechanical devices for overcoming their disability—devices from the employment of which their wives would have shrunk in disgust. In fact, few men would care to suggest to any respectable woman the adoption of such measures. Many of the impotent men, too, were supplied with the necessary implements and given instructions in their proper use by the brothel inmates. Among the best known of these devices are the rings, constructed of gold, silver, celluloid or rubber, which are fixed around the *corona glandis*; rubber rings which tightly clasp the base of the penis and thus enable erections to last longer; spiked and corrugated condoms; and an instrument mentioned by Kisch,[1] known as the "Schlitten", a sort of splint, which is designed to make possible the introduction into the vagina of the impotent man's semi-flaccid penis.

Prostitutes living in single rooms or in small flats rarely are able to provide anything so elaborate as was possible in the brothels. And there are other difficulties in the way. But there are some London prostitutes who have whips and other articles of punishment in their rooms for use with the numerous masochists (and, much less frequently, the sadists) who patronise them.

[1] E. Heinrich Kisch, *The Sexual Life of Woman*, 1910.

PART TWO

THE HISTORY OF PROSTITUTION

VI: PROSTITUTION AMONG SAVAGE AND PRIMITIVE RACES

PROSTITUTION in the present-day legal sense of the term is one of civilisation's sore spots. Strictly speaking, it has never existed among savage races in the sense that we know the professional prostitution of Soho or the Bowery. From this it is easy to make the facile assumption that savages are more chaste and more moral than civilised men and women. It is a contention that is often brought forward by writers on anthropology and ethnology. The lack of prostitution is looked upon as evidence of a lack of promiscuous intercourse, and as a proof of greater chastity among savages. Actually it presents no such evidence.

The apparent correlation of the absence of prostitution with the existence of chastity is due to failure to realise that in most savage races there exists a degree of promiscuity which in all but legal definition is indistinguishable from prostitution itself. When the whole available female population of a country acts as a professional harlot does in other countries, there is and there can be no such thing as professional prostitution.

To understand the position clearly, it must be borne in mind that the existence of prostitution depends upon the coincidental existence of one of two things : (1) a high respect for virginity and the woman's right to cherish it; or (2) the presence of some form of marriage.

In many savage tribes virginity is thought little of; in some it is thought nothing of at all. And, in certain cases, its existence after the coming of puberty constitutes a definite handicap, if not a disgrace. Marco Polo said that among the Tibetans no man would "on any consideration take to wife a girl who was a maid; for they say a wife is nothing worth unless she has been used to consort with men." According to Westermarck, among the Akamba tribe in East Africa a pregnant girl is regarded as "a most eligible spouse"; and among the Mongwandis of the Upper Mongala and the Bagas of French Guinea, men intending marriage preferred to have as their wives girls who had already given birth to children.[1] Among many savage races in different parts of the world the very fact of a woman having been the lover of many men is a great asset to her in securing a husband. The man who marries such a woman looks upon her as a most desirable creature seeing that she has attracted the attentions of so many other men.

Marriage in the civilised sense has always been preceded by communal marriage or polyandry, where the women of the race or tribe are, for the purpose of sexual intercourse, the common property of the males. Here, there is no individual property right in the woman, and actually this communal marriage is almost equivalent to what, in more civilised states, is termed prostitution. According to Theopompus, "among the Tyrrhenians it was a law that the women were common property."

With the coming into existence of any form of monogamous union, prostitution is an inevitable aftermath. The polygamous nature of man on the one hand and the surplusage of women on the other, render it, as we have seen, a universal concomitant.

Among certain tribes of the Indians of North America

[1] Edward Westermarck, *The History of Human Marriage*, fifth edition, Vol. 1 (Macmillan).

marriage (if such it can be called) was little different from promiscuity. Many a maiden, when it became sufficiently obvious that any prospects of marriage were remote, and a suitable opportunity presented itself, such as a feast or other assembly, would invite the bucks of the tribe in turn to have intercourse with her. So far from this practice causing the girl to be despised by those wishing to marry, it usually induced one of them to ask her to be his wife.

In many parts of Africa, notably in Dahomey, the custom whereby the king has the right to have intercourse with every woman is really a form of prostitution. Concubines are common, and chiefs, medicine men and other highly placed dignitaries have the right to take as many wives or concubines as they think fit. Women are bought and discarded at a moment's notice, and the majority of these become harlots in every sense of the term, selling their sexual charms to all comers.

Much of the promiscuity among savage and semi-civilised races is developed into actual prostitution by the traders, sailors and even the missionaries who come into contact with the natives. From accounts by travellers and explorers of life in various remote parts of the world, it is evident that European sailors, traders and missionaries were accustomed to hire native women to become their "temporary wives." Neither the women themselves nor their parents or husbands saw anything degrading in these promiscuous associations with foreign men. It was undoubtedly in this way that commercial prostitution and brothels came to be established in many savage or semi-civilised countries. Mayhew and Hemyng, in *London Labour and the London Poor,* dealing with prostitution among the Maoris of New Zealand, and referring to Jerningham Wakefield's description of the arrival of whalers in New Zealand ports, say: "He mentions as one of the most important transactions following this event the providing of the company with 'wives for the season.' Some had regular help-mates, but others were forced to hire women. Bargains were formally struck, and when a woman failed to give satisfaction she was exchanged for another."[1] The same writers mention that "In the criminal calendar of Wellington for 1846 we find one native convicted and punished for keeping a house of ill-fame."[2]

As money or its equivalent enters into the thing, prostitution tends to develop. In all countries and in all races there are for the finding parents who are perfectly willing to prostitute their daughters for money, and the daughters themselves, as they reach puberty, are in many instances willing to sacrifice their virginity for presents or cash. Westermarck quotes Porter[3] as saying that the girls of Madison Island (one of the Marquesas group) "are the wives of all who can purchase their favours, and a handsome daughter is considered by her parents as a blessing which secures to them, for a time, wealth and abundance."

Similarly, "among the Line Islanders of the Gilbert Group ... a woman was at liberty to accept as many men as would take her, provided they paid for the privilege."[4] Westermarck also gives instances, culled from the writings of various authorities, of the loaning out for money of their daughters and wives developing into professional harlotry among native races in various parts of the world, notably in the Melanesian Islands, in the Caroline Islands, in Uganda, in Greenland, and among numerous Indian tribes of North, Central and South America.

Many girls, too, either of their own free will or in response to

[1] Mayhew, *London Labour and the London Poor*, Extra volume, Griffin, Bohn, 1862, p. 75.

[2] *Ibid.*, p. 75.

[3] Porter, *Journal of a Cruise made in the Pacific Ocean.*

[4] Tutuila, "Line Islanders" in *Journal of the Polynesian Society*, i, 270, quoted by Westermarck, *The History of Human Marriage.*

parental instructions, adopted the role of temporary prostitute in order to earn a marriage dowry. Brantôme mentions this custom being prevalent in the olden days among the women of Cyprus, who betook themselves to the shore and earned money from the sailors calling at the island. In Nicaragua a similar custom was prevalent.

Among some tribes it is customary for men to cause their wives or daughters to have intercourse with strangers, usually in return for a reward, though in certain cases the practice has all the hallmarks of a religious rite. Thus, according to Purchas, in Caindu (the ancient name for a territory adjacent to Tibet), in honour of their gods, wives, sisters and daughters were all commanded to give themselves to travellers passing through the country.[1] In Patagonia, too, "at the command of a wizard, a man orders his wife to go to an appointed place, usually a wood, and abandon herself to the first person she meets."[2] Malinowski, in his monumental work *The Sexual Life of Savages in North-Western Melanesia*, avers that a chief named Sinakadi prostituted his wives to white men, and that at the time of publication (1929) one of his sons, a young man, was following his father's example. "A white trader," says Malinowski, "told me that he knew a native who seemed very much attached to and extremely jealous of his comely young wife. The native used to procure girls for the trader. On one occasion when he was unable to find anyone else he brought his wife, and waited for her on the doorstep."[3]

In many primitive and semi-civilised tribes it has been, and it still is, in some cases, customary to select for the specific purpose of providing sexual pleasure certain women and men. That these individuals are not termed prostitutes does not

---

[1] Quoted by J. G. Bourke in *Scatalogic Rites of All Nations*, p. 407.
[2] *Ibid.*, p. 407.
[3] Bronislaw Malinowski, *The Sexual Life of Savages in North-Western Melanesia*, Routledge, 1929, p. 272.

alter the fact that in everything else except name they are equivalent to the inmates of the more depraved and licentious of the South American brothels. Thus among the Tanni Islanders of Polynesia, a number of girls are reserved and trained in every form of sexual perversion. Perhaps, however, the most notorious of such practices was that referred to by Hammond in relation to his study of the Pueblo Indians of New Mexico. In each village it was customary for one young male to be selected for use as a pathic by all the other males. He was termed a *mujerado,* which means literally "changed into a woman."[1]

[1] W. A. Hammond, *Sexual Impotence in the Male and Female,* Davis, Detroit, 1887, p. 163.

VII: RELIGIOUS PROSTITUTION

IN its earlier phases prostitution was always associated with religion; and there seems strong ground for the assumption that the first brothels were run by priests. But instead of being called brothels they were described as temples, and their inmates, instead of being dubbed prostitutes, were referred to as daughters of the temple, priestesses of Venus, or in other euphemistic terms.

The origin of religious prostitution has been the subject of much speculation and various hypotheses have been formulated to account for it. Many early anthropologists looked upon it as a form of fertility cult, arguing that the promiscuous unions of men and women at certain festivals were thought to have marked effects upon, and to be essential to, the fertility of animals and productiveness of the land. With the coming of monogamous marriage and the consequent decline of promiscuity, it became necessary to segregate a certain proportion of the female population for these essential fertility cults. These women, who sacrificed their virginity and their right to marriage, were looked upon much in the way that we today are accustomed to look upon nuns and priests who, in the service of God, eschew all rights to the sexual pleasures and amenities of normal life.

This fertility-rite hypothesis, however, though conceivably

it may have applied in certain instances, is much too narrow to serve as a universal explanation of the origin of religious or sacred prostitution. It certainly can have had no connection with the origin of male prostitution, which, in those early days, was as widespread and as intimately connected with religion as was female prostitution.

There would seem to be far stronger ground for assuming that religious prostitution was an outcome of the beliefs, common to almost every ancient race, that sexual intercourse with a god, or with anyone intimately associated or connected with a god, was beneficial to the human participator.[1] This explanation accounts for the practice in some countries of every female assuming, with neither shame nor reluctance, the role of temporary harlot, and of no stigma attaching to this in the eyes of either her female or male compatriots.

Thus, according to Herodotus,[2] the women of Babylonia were required to sit in the temple of Mylitta until some men claimed the right to have intercourse with them. In other words, each woman was required to become a temporary prostitute, the fee paid by the man constituting an offering to the goddess presiding over the temple. Each woman was required to remain in the temple until some man selected her—the plain and the ugly were often compelled to remain for months and sometimes years on end before the act of prostitution released them. Nor was this any isolated instance—it merely stands out because Herodotus described it in such detail. There are, it is true, some who affirm that the account of Herodotus is fictitious, but these critics have overlooked the fact that there are for the finding confirmatory statements by contemporary observers. The scribes responsible for the

[1] According to Westermarck (*The History of Human Marriage*): "In Morocco, supernatural benefits are to this day expected not only from heterosexual but also from homosexual intercourse with a holy person."

[2] Herodotus, Book I, Ch. cxcix.

Epistle of Jeremy, which is one of the books of the Apocrypha, say: "It is said that the Babylonian women with cords about them sit in the ways, burning bran for incense; but if any of them, drawn by some that passeth by, be with him, she reproacheth her fellow, that she was not thought as worthy as herself, nor her cord broken."

Herodotus also refers to a similar temple in Corinth; Juvenal asserts that the Roman temples were all licensed brothels; and customs requiring females to act as temporary prostitutes in the service of the goddesses were frequent in many parts of Asia and Africa. In other instances permanent prostitutes were attached to the temples. Strabo, a contemporary historian, referring to the Temple of Aphrodite Porne at Corinth, says it contained over one hundred *hetæræ,* all of whom were required to serve the goddess. Sumner says that "under the Cæsars the most beautiful girl of the noble families of Thebes was chosen to be consecrated in the temple of Ammon. She gained honour and profit by the life of a courtesan and always found a grand marriage when she retired on account of age."[1] The dancing-girls who, until recently, were openly attached to so many temples in India were prostitutes who had intercourse when required with the priests and other temple officials, and with visitors for payment. For generations it was the custom in many parts of India for every first-born female child to be dedicated to the tribal god, to whom she was supposed to be married, and made to serve as a temple prostitute. How far this and other analogous customs survive today is almost impossible to discover. Under British rule efforts were made to stamp out temple prostitution, but there are reasons for believing that it still exists in modified and surreptitious forms. Among some of the West African tribes certain girls are not allowed to marry. They are, like the nuns in more civilised countries, dedicated to the service of their

[1] W. G. Sumner, *Folkways,* Ginn & Co., Boston, 1907, p. 541.

god and known as priestesses consecrated to the deity.[1] In all but name they are prostitutes. As such they serve the priests attached to the tribe, and, in addition, any other men willing to pay for their services in the form of a gift to the god. According to Westermarck,[2] certain female members of the Eiwe-speaking tribes of the Slave Coast, who are dedicated to the god, are in reality prostitutes, though this is in no way anything to merit reproach, every act of licentiousness of which they are guilty being looked upon as directed by their god. Similarly, on the Gold Coast (now Ghana), the priestesses were forbidden to marry, but might have sexual intercourse with any man they desired, having a right of choice analogous to the *jus primae noctis* exercised in so many countries by kings and priests.

A solitary act of prostitution, where the virgin girl is deflowered by a priest or other holy person representing the god to whom she is offering her virginity, or by a stranger, had its origin in the fear of harm resulting on the occasion of his first sexual intercourse with his bride to a man who married a virgin. This belief was widespread among ancient races, and to this day is not unknown in certain primitive or savage tribes. It was this almost universal disinclination or fear on the part of the bridegroom to deflower a virgin wife, at any rate by sexual intercourse, that led to the institution of the *jus primae noctis,* that curious and barbarous custom where the defloration of every bride was conceded to be the right of the king, or the chief, or the priest, or the medicine-man,

[1] This pagan belief is paralleled by the early Christian dedication of virgins to God and Christ and the belief that the Lord had intercourse with these "consecrated" women. The only difference is that while the "consecrated" pagans were prostitutes, the Christian "consecrated" women were the brides of God and Christ. This belief was in accordance with the early Christian concept of celibacy.

[2] Edward Westermarck, *The Origin and Development of the Moral Ideas*, Macmillan, 1917.

according to the nature of the State or the tribe or the race in question. It is customary for modern observers to look upon the *jus primae noctis* as a cruel right exercised by all-powerful rulers, and strongly resented by those who were compelled to submit to it. This was certainly true in the later years of its survival. But originally the right was gladly given, and the bridegroom, far from resenting the deflowering of his virgin wife, made every effort to find someone willing to perform the act of defloration.[1] That he was misled by the crafty priests of the day intent upon finding an excuse for the satisfying of their carnal appetites does not affect the point. He believed most firmly that harm would surely come to him if he ruptured the hymen himself; just as today thousands of persons believe that any attempt to prevent conception is a sin in the eyes of God.

There is justification for the assumption that much of the fear connected with the art of defloration was due to the haemorrhage which accompanies the rupturing of the hymenal membrane—a fear analogous to that associated with the menstrual discharge. For in many cases the blood resulting from a first coitus, like menstrual blood, was deemed to be poisonous to ordinary mortals. Only holy persons, such as the priests of god, or chiefs and kings, could deflower a virgin girl with impunity. True, occasionally, foreigners or men of other

[1] In certain cases defloration was accomplished without coitus. In Samoa, according to Krama, the bridegroom destroys the hymen with his forefinger; in other instances a stick or a skewer is used; in the Philippines the act of defloration is accomplished by one of the old women of the tribe; in India the stone, ivory or wooden phallus of an idol or god is used to rupture the hymen. A similar custom was prevalent among the Moabites, the pagan worshippers of Baal-peor, referred to so often in the Old Testament. The priestesses or prostitutes serving the god Baal had their hymens ruptured on the stone phallus of the idols which were to be found in all the temple-brothels.

tribes, supposedly immune from danger,[1] were induced to perform the act of defloration. In other instances, they were often paid to run the risk—a risk by the way which applied more specifically to the bridegroom, who was supposed to be at this time in his life peculiarly likely to be the victim of evil influences.

In certain tribes the *jus primae noctis* becomes an occasion for what in other and in all civilised races would be termed incest. The right of defloration belongs to the father of the virgin girl. Westermarck gives instances of this custom, quoting the statements of a seventeenth-century writer named Herfort that among the Sinhalese it was usual for the father to deflower his own daughter on the eve of her marriage, on the ground of "having a right to the first fruit of the tree he had planted." A similar custom was observed in certain Malayan tribes.

In other instances where no specific persons are given the right of defloration, the *jus primae noctis* is openly offered for sale. Westermarck instances the custom among the Mfiote, a tribe inhabiting the coast of Loango, of dressing up girls who have reached puberty and hawking them round from village to village. Roth, Spencer and Gillen, and other authorities, state that in many Australian aboriginal tribes each young woman on arrival at puberty is carried into the bush and forced to submit to coitus with a number of young bucks. It is a tribal custom that before any girl becomes the exclusive property of one man she must submit, after crude initiative laceration of the vagina, to promiscuous sexual intercourse with a number of selected males.

It is easy to see that from the sale or grant of the *jus*

[1] Westermarck, in *History of Human Marriage*, and Hartland, in *Ritual and Belief*, state that in many races a stranger was looked upon as a sort of semi-supernatural being, on a par with a priest or holy man, with whom intercourse was not only free from all risk to the man but also beneficial to the woman.

primae noctis, in accordance with tribal laws and superstitious observances, the step towards religious prostitution as a temporary or permanent profession is but a small one. There is a passage in *The Testament of Judah* in which it is stated that "it was a law of the Amorites that she who was about to marry should sit in fornication seven days by the gate."[1]

This practice in turn led to the giving of part of their earnings to the temple, possibly to placate the priests, and the retention of part for themselves. In India, in addition to the dancing girls dedicated to a life's servitude to the god of the temple, there were other harlots who retained part of their earnings for themselves.

Nunneries were at one time openly associated with prostitution, in many of those flourishing in the Middle Ages the inmates being little removed from the sacred prostitutes of earlier times and of primitive races. In Lisbon the nunneries were rendezvous for those given to promiscuity. In a work entitled *Authentic Memoirs Concerning the Portuguese Inquisition,* published in 1769, appears the following passage: "The king himself (John V) kept one of these consecrated vestals as a mistress, and went in publicly to her, in the face of the whole city, having built an apartment for this purpose adjoining the nunnery. However, as the custom I am speaking of gave infinite scandal to all serious people, his Majesty could do no less than put some stop to it; and, in order to terrify future delinquents, he passed the famous edict, entitled *Contra Freiraticos,* i.e. against such as carry on illicit amours with nuns." The same author states that it was no uncommon thing for the prostitutes of Lisbon to be repeating *Ave Marias* and *Pater Nosters* on their long strings of beads while engaged in their profession. He says: "Thus I can aver on my own knowledge that I never saw one of these *filles de joie* in the

---

[1] *Testaments of the Twelve Patriarchs,* translated by Charles.

street, or at a window, without her string of beads and crucifix, wherein she was mumbling her prayers."[1]

In any consideration of religious prostitution one must not overlook the fact that in some cases certainly and in many cases probably, the cloak of religion was used to excuse, justify or camouflage what was nothing but licentiousness of the most shameless brand. It would be difficult indeed to name any form of sexual vice, from promiscuity to perversions of the most loathsome type, that has not, under some euphemised name or other, been sanctioned and upheld by religion. And this is by no means restricted to ancient pagan or savage forms of religion. The polygamy of the Mormons, the unorthodox sexual practices of the Oneida Community, are examples in comparatively recent times and in civilised countries; the obscene and perverse rites which characterise the devil worshippers of Paris and London are examples in our own day.

[1] There are of course for the finding today prostitutes in Catholic countries who have a crucifix hanging on the wall, by the bed on which they are performing.

VIII: PROSTITUTION IN THE BIBLE

THE Bible, and particularly the Old Testament, contains a good many references to, and a certain amount of information about, prostitution before the advent of Christianity. In the opinion of theologians and moralists it contains too much information, and there are religious teachers, clergymen and others, who hurriedly turn over certain scandalous pages and omit certain erotic passages when reading from the Sacred Books for the edification of the young and the unsaved. As long ago as the days of Saint Jerome, the young were forbidden to have access to the Book of Ezekiel; and even today, divorced from their context, I have an idea that the descriptions of the whoredoms of Aholah and Aholibah would be put down by the moralists as rank pornography.

At that particular period with which the Old Testament deals, consorting with prostitutes appears, from all the available evidence, to have been looked upon much as in civilised countries it is looked upon today—or perhaps it would be more correct to say that, after all these centuries, apart from the fortuitous spasms of persecution and attempted repression which we shall consider in another chapter, there has been no appreciable alteration in the reaction of society as a whole to prostitution. Publicly the prostitute was denounced, just as she is today; privately she was supported and encouraged.

Of this denunciation the Bible gives many instances. Thus Solomon denounced her in the following terms:

"My son, keep my words, and lay up my commandments with thee. Keep my commandments, and live; and my law as the apple of thine eye. Bind them upon thy fingers, write them upon the table of thine heart. Say unto wisdom, Thou art my sister; and call understanding thy kinswoman: That they may keep thee from the strange woman, from the stranger which flattereth with her words. For at the window of my house I looked through my casement, and beheld among the simple ones, I discerned among the youths, a young man void of understanding. Passing through the street near her corner; and he went the way to her house, In the twilight, in the evening, in the black and dark night: And, behold, there met him a woman with the attire of an harlot, and subtile of heart. (She is loud and stubborn; her feet abide not in her house: Now is she without, now in the streets, and lieth in wait at every corner.) So she caught him, and kissed him, and with an impudent face said unto him, I have peace-offerings with me; this day have I paid my vows. Therefore came I forth to meet thee, diligently to seek thy face, and I have found thee. I have decked my bed with coverings of tapestry, with carved works, with fine linen of Egypt. I have perfumed my bed with myrrh, aloes, and cinnamon. Come, let us take our fill of love until the morning; let us solace ourselves with loves. For the good man is not at home, he is gone a long journey. He hath taken a bag of money with him, and will come home at the day appointed. With her much fair speech she caused him to yield, with the flattering of her lips she forced him. He goeth after her straightway, as an ox goeth to the slaughter, or as a fool to the correction of the stocks; Till a dart strike through his liver; as a bird hasteth to the snare, and knoweth not that it is for his life. Hearken unto me now therefore, O ye children, and attend to the words of my mouth. Let not thine heart decline to her ways, go not astray in her paths. For she hath cast down many wounded: yea, many strong men have been slain by her. Her house is the way to hell, going down to the chambers of death."

And yet Solomon's famous temple, ornamented with phallic symbols, harbouring sodomites and whores, was nothing but a brothel, in which perversions associated with the worship of Baal and Moloch, and so vigorously denounced in the Sacred Books, were surreptitiously practised, and Solomon himself, in common with other Biblical kings, had mistresses and concubines numbering many hundreds. The widow Tamar, in an attempt to secure for herself a husband, assumed the attire of a prostitute.

It was Moses, spokesman for Jehovah, who railed at the idea of prostitution: "Do not prostitute thy daughter, to cause her to be a whore; lest the land fall to whoredom, and the land become full of wickedness" (Leviticus xix. 29). And again: "There shall be no whore of the daughters of Israel, nor a sodomite of the sons of Israel. Thou shalt not bring the hire of a whore, or the price of a dog, into the house of the Lord thy God for any vow: for even both these are abomination unto the Lord thy God" (Deuteronomy xxiii. 17-18). Yet he took no actual prohibitory measures against the cohabitation of young men with prostitutes from other lands.

Most of the old Hebrew prophets and lawmakers themselves patronised harlots, and looked upon such escapades as the mildest of peccadilloes. As an instance, the powerful and wealthy Judah, praised and worshipped by his brethren,[1] slept

---

[1] "Judah, thou art he whom thy brethren shall praise: thy hand shall be in the neck of thine enemies; thy father's children shall bow down before thee" (Genesis xlix, 8).

with a harlot[1] and made no secret of the fact. Jephthah, the Gileadite,[2] who was a judge in Israel for six years, was the son of a prostitute. In short, promiscuous sexual relations on the part of men, so long as they were not unduly advertised, came in for little in the way of censure. But the woman caught in adultery, or pursuing the profession of the harlot, was denounced, harassed and punished. It was the universal attitude of man towards woman asserting itself. Women, other than his own relatives, were to be pursued and seduced. Hence to preserve as much as possible the chastity of his female adherents, the punishments for adultery or fornication on the part of the married or betrothed woman were enacted; the harsh stipulation against prostitution within the race; the command against the employment of prostitutes in the temples.

When we come to consider the many references to male prostitution in the Old Testament we see an entire change of attitude, and the new attitude here expressed has dominated the reaction of society towards sodomy and its analogues in all Christian countries through the ages. We have seen that female prostitutes were attached, under various euphemistic names, to most of the temples throughout the then known world, and that the Hebrew temples were no exceptions. But in certain races, worshipping gods other than Jehovah, male prostitutes also were attached to the temples. The vehemence with which sodomy was denounced by the Hebrews was due more to the fact that it was a feature of a rival and so-called heretical religion than because of the practice itself. Westermarck has pointed out that "the word *Kādēsh,* translated 'sodomite,' properly denotes a man dedicated to a deity; and it appears that such men were consecrated to the mother of the gods, the famous Dea Syria, whose priests or devotees they

[1] Genesis xxxviii. 18.
[2] Judges xi. 1.

were considered to be."[1] The sin which, according to the Hebrew ideology, towered above every other sin was disbelief in the Lord God Jehovah and the worshipping of other gods. The first commandment was essentially the most important. It was natural that the mere fact that worshippers of rival gods practised sodomy should lead the Hebrews to give to the world this explanation as their justification for a policy of rigorous persecution and oppression. Sodom and Gomorrah were destroyed primarily because they were the seats of heretical cults, of which the practice of unnatural sexual vice was only one feature. Thus connotations between idolatry and sodomy were established, and we see the recurrent denunciation which runs through the Bible:

"Thou shalt not lie with mankind as with womankind: it is abomination" (Leviticus xviii. 22).

"If a man also lie with mankind as he lieth with a woman, both of them have committed an abomination: they shall surely be put to death; their blood shall be upon them" (Leviticus xx. 13).

"And there were also sodomites in the land, and they did according to all the abominations of the nations which the Lord cast out before the children of Israel" (I Kings xiv. 24).

With the coming of Christianity the sex act, in any form, and whether committed in wedlock or otherwise, was denounced. The dour and ascetic Saint Paul glorified celibacy and chastity until they became prominent features of the early Christian religion. It was this outlook on sex which led to the rule that no man or woman, married or unmarried, who had performed the sex act the previous night should take part in a Church festival or in the Eucharist.

[1] Edward Westermarck, *The Origin and Development of the Moral Ideas.*

At the same time there was a change from the relentless and sadistic cruelty which was so marked a feature of the Mosaic code; and the adulterer and the prostitute were no longer hounded to death for their sins. The teaching of Christ was mainly one of forgiveness and charity. We see this well exemplified in his treatment of the harlot:

"And the scribes and Pharisees brought unto him a woman taken in adultery; and when they had set her in the midst, They say unto him, Master, this woman was taken in adultery, in the very act. Now Moses in the law commanded us, that such should be stoned; but what sayest thou? This they said, tempting him, that they might have to accuse him. But Jesus stooped down, and with his finger wrote on the ground, as though he heard them not. So, when they continued asking him, he lifted up himself, and said unto them, He that is without sin among you, let him first cast a stone at her. And again he stooped down, and wrote on the ground. And they which heard it, being convicted by their own conscience, went out one by one, beginning at the eldest, even unto the last: and Jesus was left alone, and the woman standing in the midst. When Jesus had lifted up himself, and saw none but the woman, he said unto her, Woman, where are those thine accusers? hath no man condemned thee? She said, No man, Lord. And Jesus said unto her, Neither do I condemn thee: go, and sin no more" (John viii. 3-11).

IX: DEVELOPMENT OF PROSTITUTION
UNDER CIVILISATION

WHEN once religious prostitution had been definitely established it was bound in time to develop into professional prostitution as we know it today, and as every country in which monogamous marriage is an institution has known it, every step that is made to tighten up monogamy and, coincidentally, to ostracise free love, is bound to develop prostitution. So much so, indeed, that the growth of prostitution inevitably follows the path of the missionary in savage and semi-civilised countries.

We can trace the growth of prostitution step by step. First we have the promiscuity of savages; next religious or sacred prostitution; finally professional harlotry, which may be either of the free-lance kind or brothel prostitution. Often one form was so intermixed with another, or was carried on under a religious aegis for the sake of appearances, that it is difficult to discover where exactly religious prostitution finished and professional prostitution began. The monetary aspect entered into it, however, whatever may have been the ostensible reason offered. According to Herodotus, the Pyramids were built out of money derived from prostitution, Cheops going so far as to drive his own daughter into the profession in order to build the Pyramid that bears his name. Actually, in most cases, the temple harlots, when commandeered by other tribes, were forced to ply their profession in the capacity of slaves in public brothels.

The attitude of the male population of ancient Greece to the prostitute is full of significance, and worthy of more than passing attention. Moreover, it is not without its parallels, as we shall see later, in modern civilisation. Women, respectable women—that is, wives, daughters and relatives—were looked upon as so many pieces of property, much as the furniture, the house and the farm livestock were looked upon. It was the old property right of man *vis-à-vis* woman functioning in all its glory, as it was to continue to function for four thousand years. The place for a wife, in the full literal significance of the term, was in her home. Her function in life was to look after the household, to procreate children and to rear them. And while the respectable married woman, virtuous to a degree, went about her menial duties, her lord and husband flaunted away his leisure hours in the company of painted women of joy. In all this, it may be argued, there was nothing that is not customary at the present day; which is true enough, except that in ancient Greece there was nothing secret or surreptitious in the practices—they were done quite openly. Both the men's wives and their neighbours knew all about their carryings on. More, the highest-class prostitutes, known as *hetæræ*, secured respect, attention and honour, without being compelled to have recourse to subterfuge or to disguise their true calling under euphemistic terms. The very fact that they could drive about the streets with their painted faces unveiled proclaimed to all the world exactly what they were, and shouted to the four winds of heaven that they were forbidden to take part in certain religious ceremonies, and that any children to which they happened to give birth could never rank as citizens. These *hetæræ* were the companions of the wealthiest, most cultured and most exalted Greeks of the time. They were women of beauty, education, culture and attraction, outshining in every respect the virtuous wives who were engaged in breeding and rearing the children of the race. It was one of these prostitutes, the notorious Aspasia, whose power and influence a queen might well have envied, and whose name has lived through the centuries, who was loved by Alcibiades, Socrates and by scores of others, finally marrying Pericles. Another, by name Bacchis, was the mistress of Hyperides; yet another, known as Thargelia, was the lover and confidant of Xerxes; Archaeanassa was the mistress of Plato; Gnathena lived with Dyphiles; Phryne had among her numberless lovers Hyperides, Apelles and Praxiteles. And there were others and again others—the list is endless.

Of course only the most wealthy and influential citizens could afford to consort with these *hetæræ*, whose gorgeous upholstery and costly establishments required the bank roll of a millionaire. Demosthenes lavished his fortune on Lais; on Pythionice the wealth of Babylon was squandered.

The ordinary citizens of Greece had to be content with prostitutes of less charm, and these were looked upon and treated in an altogether different manner from the aristocratic *hetæræ*. The temple of Venus at Corinth, which housed a full thousand *dicteriades* or common prostitutes, and similar temples in Athens and other cities, catered for the sexual wants of the sailors who thronged every port and every town. Here every form of sexual depravity was obtainable at low cost.

The first public brothel of which we have any record was the one which Solon established in Athens.[1] The inmates were slaves, receiving nothing for their services beyond food and clothing, the fees paid to them going to the State. These whore-houses were known as *dicteria,* and the women who inhabited them as *dicteriades.* Some idea of the number of

---

[1] Solon justified his action on the ground that prostitution, though an evil, was an essential evil. Incidentally he amassed vast wealth through this project.

men who had recourse to the brothels for their sexual requirements is indicated by the fact that out of the profits made through the *dicteria* a large and ornate temple was built.

Much the same custom seems to have been prevalent throughout the whole of ancient Greece, though the regulations imposed by Solon were modified and gradually the prostitute emerged from her one-time slave-like position. But she was compelled to pay taxes to the State. The *dicteriades* remained the lowest class of prostitutes, frequenting the port of Athens, and repairing to the nearest *dicteria,* or to any nearby spot sheltered from the public gaze, with whoever were willing to pay the small fixed price. There appear to have been few restrictions as regards the running of these public brothels. Anyone who could pay the State tax was allowed to open a *dicterion.* So much for the common prostitutes, who were on a par with those found in the lowest type of South American seaport brothel of the present day.

The female flute-players and dancing girls, known as *auletrides,* were of a much superior class to the common prostitute—superior, that is, in dress, in speech, in bearing. They were engaged at all the banquets, festivals, and suchlike entertainments, public and private; they were accomplished professional musicians and entertainers. Providing music for the guests was, however, but a small, and a minor, part of the entertainment which these *auletrides* were called upon to furnish. They had to satisfy other appetites. There can be little doubt, judging from references in the works of Athenæus, Lucian, Antiphanes and contemporary writers, that every form of sexual depravity was pandered to by these girls; and that these sexual excesses were not confined to men. Tribadism, also, formed a part of erotic repertoire. The more talented and beautiful of these flute-players were often the lovers of celebrated and powerful men. The famous and notorious Lamia became the mistress of Demetrius, and was deified Venus Lamia after having fabulous wealth lavished upon her and a temple built in her honour.

Turning from ancient Greece to Rome, we find constant references to prostitution in the works of the oldest historians and litterateurs.[1] And we find, too, the outlook on prostitution of the inhabitants of Rome, all those thousands of years ago, in close accord with the outlook of England today. Unlike the Greeks, the Romans were ashamed to be seen in open companionship with avowed harlots—they skulked and sneaked into the brothels or houses of assignation unknown to their friends and relatives, much in the way in which a respectable man of the first half of the twentieth century made overtures to a *fille de joie* in one of the darker and less frequented side-streets of the Leicester Square district.

Under Roman law we find the earliest attempts at registration of prostitutes, there being in force a system of inscribing known professional public women similar in its general principles to that in force in certain countries today. Indeed, the main difference appears to be that in Rome there was no attempt at medical examination, and it is probable that at that time there was no traceable connection whatever between prostitution and the spread of venereal infection: in fact we have no actual evidence that either syphilis or gonorrhoea were prevalent, or, if prevalent, that they were recognised as diseases of venery.

"Once a prostitute, always a prostitute" was the dictum of the Roman authorities. In other words, if a girl was inscribed as a public prostitute, the giving up of her profession for any reason whatever did not constitute grounds for the removal of her name from the register. These registered harlots were compelled to wear clothes of a specified uniform type, and to dye their hair yellow or red or blue.[2] All these and other regula-

[1] See Martial, Plautus, Lacantius and Tacitus.

[2] This rule did not apply to the inmates of brothels.

tions were ostensibly designed to discourage girls from taking up the profession, and to degrade in every possible way those who did elect to become prostitutes.[1]

It is one thing to pass laws dealing with so amorphous and so universal a thing as prostitution; it is quite another thing to enforce them. And a study of the writings of the Roman historians reveals the fact that there was a very considerable number of prostitutes who practised their profession while managing to evade registration, and in this way, in addition to escaping the branding iron, they evaded payment of taxes which were collected from their inscribed sisters.

Most of the registered prostitutes practised their profession in brothels, or *lupanaria,* as they were called. They were either inmates permanently or temporarily hired by the owner of the brothel; or they were street women who rented a room or cell in a brothel when they required the use of it. But by no means all the prostitutes used the brothels. Registered women were not compelled to inhabit *lupanaria.* They could receive their clients in private houses provided they affixed on the doors the nature of their profession and their fees. The unregistered prostitutes naturally enough could not use the brothels without standing self-confessed as violators of the law, and so they were compelled to use houses where no questions were asked, or to indulge in intercourse in the open, a practice which involved little risk of detection owing to the fact that, in those days, there was no such thing as any form of artificial street-lighting.

In addition to the uninscribed common harlots there were, as there have been wherever prostitution has flourished, certain females indistinguishable in appearance and in manners

[1] The real reason behind the wearing of special garments was not *always* with a view to debasing the career of the prostitute, though this may have been paraded to the world. In many cases its sole object was to help the male population to distinguish the women of easy compliance from their more respectable sisters.

from women of respectability, who managed to conceal their true profession from the public. They mixed with the fashionable society of ancient Rome, they had slaves to attend their wants. These were ostensibly the mistresses of the powerful governors and rulers of the Empire. They were prostitutes of this stamp who ministered to the sensual appetites of Nero, of Vitellius, of Vespasian, of Severus, of Titus, of Domitian and others. Incest, too, was rife. Domitian had sexual intercourse with his niece; Nero committed incest with his own sisters. So, too, did Commodus, whose palace was a brothel populated with three hundred of the most beautiful girls of the age, Elagabalus, pervert and sexual monster, mingled naked with the palace harlots day and night.

Mention of prostitution under the aegis of the Romans would be incomplete without some reference to the early Christians, who practised their religion as much as possible in secret. It is a fact common to all countries in which prostitution is officially and publicly frowned upon that members of the male population view the harlots of foreign or heretical origin with much more complacency than erring females of their own race or religion. The raping of women has always been a part of the persecution meted out to enemy or inferior nations or races in times of both peace and war, and in both savage and civilised countries. According to Suetonius, all virgins who were condemned to death in ancient Rome were raped by the executioner before he performed his task. No surprise need be felt then at the practice of compelling Christian virgins, whenever they were discovered, to enter the public brothels. This practice also does something to explain the fact that it was under the aegis of the Christian religion that the beginning of a more charitable and tolerant outlook upon prostitution[1] manifested itself, and the woman who had

[1] It is true that religious prostitution was looked upon not only with tolerance but with approval, but in this connection it is import-

sinned in this manner, on repentance, was allowed the benefits and privileges of the Christian religion.

The submission that prostitution was the lesser of two evils, acknowledged by many of the fathers of the Church, was the beginning of a long period of widespread toleration, which gradually extended into approval. The Roman system of regulation and licensing was adopted by one State after another until, in practically every part of Europe, there was some system whereby public women were available in certain quarters of the big cities. In many cases the State or the city benefited by the taxes which the prostitutes, or the owners of the brothels, were called upon to contribute.

In the Middle Ages, so important a part in the life of the city did the brothels become that it was customary for the city authorities to cause the more important brothels to place their inmates at the disposal of royalty, celebrities or other important guests of the city, without any charge. In Burchard's *Diary* occurs a description of an orgy in the private rooms of the Pope, where, after supper, fifty naked prostitutes danced for the amusement of the Pope's guests, among whom were the notorious Cæsar and Lucrezia Borgia. At this time a considerable portion of the Pope's income consisted of a tax on brothels. This attitude, whereby the State or the city derived from the brothels considerable financial benefit, and important personages secured amusement in addition, was common throughout Europe. In 1347 Queen Johanna of Naples arranged for a city brothel at Avignon, to which free access was given to all men of rank or celebrity. On the occasion of the visit of the Emperor Sigismund to Ulm in 1434, the royal suite visited the common brothels. Every royal palace had its own brothel, and every royal tour had its accompanying band

ant to remember that at that time these temple harlots were not looked upon or known as prostitutes at all—they were "priestesses" or "wives" of the deity.

of prostitutes, too. Charles the Bold maintained a retinue of at least four thousand for the use of himself and his court. Every moving army similarly was followed by hordes of harlots. The Crusaders had thousands at their heels, each camp maintaining its own large brothel. Even the devout Francis I had a collection of "camp followers" who were paid for their services, as is shown in the royal account books. In more recent times these "camp followers," though none the less existent, have been dignified by more euphemistic names.

In these days, owing to the hypocritical attitude adopted by many governments, and especially by all English-speaking peoples, towards prostitution, such a state of affairs as prevailed in the Middle Ages appears extraordinarily vulgar and immoral. But to understand the position it must be remembered that at that time intercourse with a common prostitute, or openly visiting a brothel, was looked upon with no more reprobation than in these days one looks upon a visit to a night club or a carousal in a public-house. So ordinary and so necessary an amusement was a visit to a brothel conceded to be that it was the custom for important public dignitaries and officials, when travelling on business connected with the State, to charge, as part of their legitimate travelling expenses, the cost of visiting public brothels in the towns where they stayed the night. Some shadow of this attitude towards prostitution still persists in certain foreign States, where patronage of brothels and sleeping with harlots are both looked upon as mild peccadilloes and openly admitted. Probably, however, at no period in history have prostitutes—whose profession was openly admitted and brazenly described by its real name— ranked higher than they did in the fourteenth and fifteenth centuries. The brothels attached to the royal palaces were sumptuous apartments; the women who were chosen to grace them were, so long as they remained in favour, elegantly attired. The official who was in charge of the royal brothel, and whose duties were those of a modern pimp or procurer, far from being shunned and looked down upon as a contemptible and criminal debauchee, held considerable rank and was known as "King of the Prostitutes." His female assistant—the counterpart of the modern brothel *madame*—was similarly a court official in whom was vested much authority and dignity.

With the coming of the Reformation the policy of concealing the real profession of these women under a variety of fancy and euphemistic names flourished abundantly in all its glory. This policy was extended and developed all through the ages, reaching its higher and more decorative forms in the *demi-mondaines* and *grandes cocottes* of Italy and France; the "demi-reps" of England; and their prototypes in civilised countries the world over.

There is evidence that at one time the patrons of the brothels were entertained by professional clowns or fools. In Douce's *Illustrations of Shakspeare and of Ancient Manners,* we read: "The fool in this play (*Timon of Athens*) is a very obscure and insignificant character. Dr Johnson's conjecture that he belongs to one of Alcibiades' mistreses is extremely probable. Many ancient prints conduce to show that women of this description were attended by buffoons; and there is good reason for supposing, partly from the same kind of evidence, that in most brothels such characters were maintained to amuse the guests by their broad jokes and seasonable antics. In *Measure for Measure* we have such a person, who is also a tapster, and in *Antony and Cleopatra* (Act 1, Scene 1) we hear of a *strumpet's fool*."[1]

In the old days even many of the brothels were dignified by more polite names. Often they were called baths. In point of fact every public bath in the Middle Ages was a brothel. The connection between bathing and venery, which is well

[1] Francis Douce, *Illustrations of Shakspeare and of Ancient Manners,* Tegg, London, 1839, pp. 358-9.

known to every sexologist, was also not unknown to the ancients. As long ago as the time of Mohammed we find that old sage and law-giver saying: "All the earth is given to me as a place of prayer, and as pure, except the burial ground and the bath." The notorious "stews" (baths) of London were neither more nor less than common whore-houses.[1] They were mostly found in the Borough of Southwark, near the palace of the Bishop of Winchester, who at that time obtained a big income from the rents of these "stews." Certain regulations were imposed by Parliament respecting the conditions to be observed by those renting the brothels, and by those using them. A prostitute was compelled to lie with her mate the whole night—in no case was one of the brothels to be used as what, in more modern teminology, is called a "short-time" house. Nor was a prostitute, or the keeper of the "stew-house," allowed to entice men to enter. No woman suffering from a venereal disease ("burning")[2] was allowed to be an inmate; nor was a woman known to be married. The "stews" were searched once a week by a constable or other officer of the law. In 1545 the eighth Henry, urged on by the Reformation Party, closed the "stews" of Southwark, and thus ended England's first and only experiment in the provision of brothels for the purpose of prostitution.

The abolition of the "stews" did not mean that baths ceased to be the resorts of prostitutes and their clients: it merely meant that the bagnios no longer ranked as *licensed* or *regulated* brothels. Indeed, bath-houses became more popular than ever among the ladies of the town, and in the seven-

---

[1] The close connection between baths and promiscuity or perversion appears to have been universally recognised throughout the civilised world of those days. More recently, in 1649, the scheme of one Peter Chamberlin to build baths in all English cities failed, upon the ground of morality, to receive the sanction of Parliament.

[2] This would appear to have been the first attempt to prevent the spread of venereal infection, not only in England but in any country.

teenth and eighteenth centuries were flourishing unashamedly and in numbers throughout the capital city. Archenholz, writing in 1790, described one of these resorts in the following words: "There is in London a species of houses called bagnios, the sole intention of which is to procure pleasure. These are magnificent buildings, and the furniture contained in them is not unworthy of the palace of a prince. They there procure everything that can enrapture the senses.... This kind of entertainment is very expensive, and yet sometimes the bagnios are full all night long. For the most part, they are situated within a few paces of the theatres, or are surrounded by taverns. The profusion of wealth wasted in them occasioned Beaumarchais, who is not unacquainted with the luxuries of Paris, to affirm 'that more money is exhausted during one night in the taverns and bagnios of London than would maintain all the seven United Provinces for six months.' "[1] Some of these bagnios were attached to taverns; others were independent concerns. Of the latter perhaps the most notorious and magnificent were the Duke's Bath or Bagnio in Long Acre, afterwards renamed the King's Bagnio, and The Hummums in Covent Garden.

In no European country did prostitution grow and flourish more rapidly than in France, and by the time of the first Napoleon the position was serious indeed, leading to the passing of various measures designed specifically to deal with the evil, culminating in the registration of professional women. There were two kinds of prostitutes recognised at the time—those living in houses of prostitution (*maisons de tolérance*), and those who led a free-lance existence: both were subject to inscription. Writing in 1869, Acton describes a typical Parisian house thus: "The visitor is received by the mistress of the house, and ushered into a sumptuous anteroom; on a curtain being drawn aside, a door is revealed to him, contain-

[1] M. D. Archenholz, *A Picture of England*, Dublin, 1790, p. 195.

ing a circular piece of glass about the size of a crown piece, through which he can reconnoitre at his ease a small, but well-lighted and elegantly furnished, drawing-room, occupied by the women of the establishment. They are usually to be seen seated on sofa chairs, elegantly attired in different-coloured silks, with low bodices, and having their hair dressed in the extreme of fashion; the whole group being arranged artistically, as in a *tableau vivant,* and the individuals who comprise it representing the poses of different celebrated statues, selected apparently with the object of showing off to the best advantage the peculiar attractions of the different women. From the room of observation the visitor can, if he pleases, select his victim. . . . If this somewhat cold-blooded process of selection is distasteful to him, and he desires to become acquainted with the women in a less summary manner—or if the object of his visit is merely amusement, or the satisfaction of curiosity, without any ulterior aim—he can enter the room, and enjoy the society of its occupants, . . . all that is expected from him being to stand a reasonable amount of champagne, or other refreshment, and make himself generally agreeable." The author goes on to point out the danger inevitably associated with such a course, for a house of this nature was equipped with everything ingenuity could suggest, as well as possessing an atmosphere "calculated to captivate the senses and arouse desire." He continues "In some of these houses scenes may be witnessed which can only be enacted by women utterly dead to every sense of shame, in whom every vestige of decency has been trampled out, leaving them merely animated machines for stimulating and gratifying the basest passions."[1] So far as a good deal of the day was concerned monotonousness was the keynote of the life of the inmates.

The houses were extremely profitable, as was evidenced by

[1] William Acton, *prostitution considered in its moral, social and sanity aspects,* 1870.

the immense sums for which they frequently changed hands.
The fee charged varied, according to the type of house, from
five to twenty francs, and in most of them liquor was sold.
As regards the street girls, these, according to the above-
mentioned authority, were restricted to certain districts, and
were not allowed to solicit. Their flamboyant attire and general
appearance, however, proclaimed their calling.

Speaking of the bawdy houses of Amsterdam in the early
years of the nineteenth century, Little says they were licensed
houses, and that the girls themselves, as well as the brothel-
owners, paid a tax to the State. "To these places," he says,
"people of character resort openly, without fear or shame.
There is as little scandal in being seen in one of them as at a
playhouse, or any other place of amusement. The entertainments are music and dancing: those nymphs who are not
engaged in dancing with their paramours sit round the room;
and a stranger talks to them as long as he thinks proper, and
generally offers them wine and other refreshments, as he would
to persons at an assembly. Every man who leads out a girl to
dance pays sixpence to the music. If anyone chooses to retire
with them, there are small rooms adjoining, furnished with a
bed and other conveniences; and their return attracts not the
least notice."[1] It is worthy of note that, according to Bourke,
the prostitutes of Amsterdam were extremely superstitious,
keeping horse-dung in their rooms to bring good luck and
avert evil.[2]

The end of a long period of toleration and approval, and of
a degree of licentiousness without parallel except in ancient
history, came at last, and with it a strong reaction of feeling
against prostitution and prostitutes, resulting in wholesale attempts at suppression and punishment. From the beginning

[1] Thomas Little, *The Beauty of the Sexes*, second edition, Vol.
III, p. 17.
[2] J. G. Bourke, *Scatologic Rites of all Nations*, p. 255.

of history there had been fortuitous attempts, usually on the part of some individual ruler, to suppress or regulate prostitution, but nothing in any way like the campaign which swept the larger part of Europe in the sixteenth century. These attempts, and this changed attitude, have usually been regarded as due to a reawakening of morality and religion in the people, and especially in the men at the heads of the various countries. The assumption is an erroneous one. It was due to neither religion nor morality. It was due to fear of disease. At this time syphilis had obtained a firm hold in several European countries, and there can be little doubt that the charge brought against prostitutes and the public brothels, of extending the prevalence of the disease, though considerably exaggerated, had a good deal of truth in it. The rich, the powerful and the celebrated alike ceased to patronise the brothels, and, once these personages were no longer personally interested in the dens of vice as sources of amusement and of revenue, they were willing to don the reformer's cloak and give heed to the outcry against prostitution and the women connected with it. State and Church united in a harrying of these unfortunate women which at times reached unparalleled levels of cruelty.

X: HISTORICAL ASPECTS OF PROSTITUTION IN THE UNITED KINGDOM

BRITAIN has always had its prostitutes. Also, as in every other civilised country, the profession of prostitution has had its ups and downs. At times these women of easy virtue have displayed unparalleled brazenness; at other times they have, to all intents and purposes, disappeared from the streets. Such vicissitudes have reflected the increased or decreased toleration displayed by the authorities as a result of public clamour or the activities of religious associations.

The bagnios of London and many other provincial cities of Britain were at one time notorious. In many cases they were run by prostitutes who had ceased to hawk their own bodies, probably in most cases having discovered that it was far more profitable as well as more conducive to health to merchant the bodies of others. Also in many cases they had little choice in the matter, being themselves too old or too unattractive to secure clients.

Some of these brothels were luxurious in their appointments, appealing to a wealthy clientele. Others were poor affairs. Mostly, they were houses of a size sufficient to accommodate from six to a dozen inmates, situated in London and the larger provincial cities and towns. Occasionally they took bizarre forms. An eighteenth-century brothel of a most unusual type, known as "The Folly," was described in the

European Magazine as "a very large vessel said to have been the hulk of a ship of war or frigate, which was moored on the Surrey side of the Thames, nearly opposite Hungerford Stairs, and, consequently, abreast of Cooper's Gardens. It was used as a floating tavern and bagnio. The proprietors had an idea that a licence was not necessary for a place of this discription on the river, and it was continued many years unrestrained, till at length its enormities became so notorious that its suppression was deemed a most necessary object of the police."[1]

James Boswell records[2] a number of encounters with prostitutes, and had intercourse with one on Westminster Bridge, remarking that "the whim of doing it there with the Thames rolling below us amused me much." Boswell, who caught venereal disease, used to pay about a shilling for his encounters, and in his day, of course, there were few lit streets and the police system was rudimentary.

An excellent description of the type of woman who ran one of London's high-class brothels, and of the inmates, is given by Pierce Egan. The period of which he writes is the early nineteenth century. "The Oxonian," which is the name given to the character who introduces Jerry and Tom to the night life of the metropolis, says:

"I mean to inform you that those three nymphs, who have so much dazzled your optics, are three nuns, and the plump female is Mother —— of great notoriety, but generally designated the Abbess of ——. Her residence is at no great distance from one of the royal palaces; and she is distinguished for her bold, ingenuous line of conduct in the profession which she has chosen to adopt; so much so, indeed, that she eclipses all her competitors in infamy.

[1] Quoted by J. P. Malcolm, *Anecdotes of London in the Eighteenth Century;* second edition, 1810, Vol. I, p. 231.
[2] See *Boswell's London Journal, 1762-1763* (Heinemann, 1950).

... Mother ——— is also very anxious to preserve something like 'a reputation'; that, when she is spoken of among the gay votaries of pleasure, it might be said, that the 'devil is never half so black as he is painted.' This desire of 'reputation,' it ought to be observed, does not originate from qualms of conscience, but arises from her peculiar sagacity to prevent interruptions to the business of her house, in order that her visitors may not be 'broken in' upon, or overhauled by the unmannerly intrusion of officers of justice, accompanied by distracted parents seeking their deluded children. It is the greatest boast of Mother ——— that she is an open and avowed enemy of seduction, also that the cries and lamentations of ruined girls shall not echo along the walls of her mansion. Her maxim is, that good order must be pre-eminent.... She is candid and sincere in her professions; and will not suffer any damsels to enter her service under any species of delusion.... She points out to them the vicissitudes they are likely to meet with in such an uncertain career; but particularly to bear in mind, that, whatever disaster may ensue, it is solely attributable to themselves. It must also be well understood, that, in connecting themselves with her household, it is entirely from their own preference and adoption! and those girls who cannot comply with her dictates had much better relinquish their intentions. Mother ——— is completely a woman of business.

She also makes known to those females who apply to her for places, that those girls who conduct themselves well will meet with every indulgence: no pleasure is denied to them; besides having the pleasure and enjoyment of an elegant carriage, and livery servants to attend upon them to all the public places of resort. But their character for honesty must bear the strictest investigation: this point, Mother ——— is very scrupulous on ascertaining: as her house is not only furnished abundantly with plate, but the trinkets necessary to be displayed on their persons, when she sends them to the opera, the theatres, masquerades, &c., require on her part some little caution. Mother ——— always pays great attention to the health of her ladies, as a son of Æsculapius belongs to the establishment. The above preliminaries being adjusted, no time is lost in conducting the 'new inmate' to a most elegant wardrobe, where the metamorphosis is soon rendered complete; and Betty, who perhaps had but recently scoured the dirty floor of some humble dwelling, now becomes the fashionable Cyprian, to take wine from the hands of a gentleman. Everything that art can devise to improve the shape; cosmetics to heighten the complexion; and dresses of the most fascinating description, to render the *tout ensemble* luxuriantly captivating, are resorted to. . . . No woman knows the taste of her visitors better than Mother ———. It is her peculiar study, and she is considered to excel in all her entertainments: but in keeping her eye towards the 'main chance' those fashionables who participate in her midnight revels will soon be taught the necessity of having a long purse. Though modesty is not the motto of Mother———, yet she is a woman of discernment and polite behaviour. She is not to be easily duped, and before she introduces her 'new inmates' to the gallants, she deems it necessary to give them a few instructions, to put them on their guard against many impositions that novices are liable to in the various walks of life. Her particular injunctions to her pupils are: 'However, my girls, you may be amused, never suffer yourselves to be bilked.' With this advice, the thoughtless girls make their appearance in her 'Show Room'; not with the coyness inherent to modesty, but with the loose manners of Bacchantes, singing:

'From tyrant laws and customs free,
We follow sweet variety.'

This apartment is particularly calculated, from its elegant
embellishments, to co-operate in setting-off to great advantage of the charms of its female visitors; and to these regions
of pleasure all the gay boys of the Town occasionally resort.
Mother ———— is indefatigable in her selection, and the
keeping up of her stock of beautiful females. An admittance
to her mansion requires but little introduction; yet her
visitors consist principally of the higher classes of society."[1]

This same literary and pictorial record gives many revealing glimpses of the methods and behaviour of the prostitutes
of that day, whether brothel *habituées,* or unattached girls
plying their trade without let or hindrance.

Depicted among the patrons of the saloon are several persons who are present for the express purpose, it is stated, of
"keeping a most vigilant eye that none of their 'decked-out
girls' brush off with the property entrusted to them for the
night."[2] In those days it was customary for prostitutes who
could not afford to buy the fashionable attire needed in their
profession to hire dresses and other habiliments, and there
was a distinct risk, in such cases, of the owners never seeing
either the goods or the girls again. Even in the case of brothel
prostitutes, it was customary for a fee to be charged for the
loan of the dresses.

The drink most favoured by these women was gin, generally
referred to as "Blue Ruin." Other contemporary writers have
referred to this predilection for gin, and one, to wit Colonel
George Hanger, gives a reason for it, remarking that it was
generally thought that this particular spirit, because of its

[1] Pierce Egan, *Life in London*, Hotten, n.d. (c. 1869).
[2] Pierce Egan, *op. cit.*

diuretic properties, was conducive to health. Says the same writer: "A physician of respectability, in this town, is of opinion, were it not for the general use of gin among the common women, one half of them would be rotten."[1]

At many of the lower-class brothels, which had no regular clientele, the visitor was lucky to escape with the payment of nothing further than the arranged fee, for in the most instances he was robbed as well. In the Leeds brothels referred to by William Logan it was computed that the proceeds of these robberies averaged half a crown a visit. There were various ways in which these robberies were effected. Often the girl "lifted" the money from her companion's person while he was asleep or drunk. In other cases a "bully" performed the same office, or induced the visitor to hand over a sum of money in circumstances amounting to blackmail or even *force majeure*. An eighteenth-century writer, Richard King, says: "Bullies are dependants on bawds and whores; sometimes the bully pretends to be the husband of the whore, whose bread he eats, whose quarrel he fights, and at whose call he is always ready to act and do as commanded. These men are persons of a vicious and disorderly life, and often have lavished their whole substance on the very women that have them in keeping, for the purposes of defending them from insults, and giving a sanction to their calling. It is a very common thing for these women to bring home a gentleman, and, on entering the house, ask the maid in a whisper 'if her master is at home?' The maid, according to her former instructions, replies no, he is gone out of town, and will not return till to-morrow; upon which the gentleman is invited in, and entertained with a story of the bully's jealousy and the whore's constancy, till matters are settled in such a manner as to make his presence necessary, which takes place

[1] *The Life, Adventures, and Opinions of Col. George Hanger*, written by himself, 1801, Vol. I, p. 154*n*.

on the gentleman's intimation of going away. The bill being called for, if he finds fault with the charge the maid enters and says her master is below, and immediately the bully appears, who demands his business there; 'if he wants to debauch his wife, or bilk the house?' Blusters, and talks of bringing an action for *crim. con.*, but at length is pacified by the bill's being discharged, and his quondam spouse satisfied."

"A countryman of my acquaintance being in town," continues King, "was lured by a young wanton on the look-out, and inveigled to a well-known bagnio in the environs of Covent Garden, where they regaled themselves for some time with the best the house afforded, when the lady proposed adjourning to her own house to spend the remaining part of the evening, a reception free from molestation. Accordingly the bill was called for and paid, and the couple retired to the lady's lodgings, where they spent the night in joy and festivity. But lo! when morning came, and my acquaintance was about to depart there was a demand of five guineas made by madam for lodging, &c., besides what you please for civility, and something for the maid. Being struck with the exorbitancy of the demand, he absolutely refused to comply therewith; upon which Mr Bully made his appearance, and in a peremptory tone insisted on the lodgings being paid, the lady satisfied, and some acknowledgment to the maid, for the extra trouble she had been at in sitting up all night to prevent his running away without discharging his fees, or he swore he would run him through the body. The countryman having a greater regard for life than money, and more self-love than courage, tamely submitted to the bully's menaces, and dropped seven guineas and a crown, for which he had a receipt on his posteriors signed by the bully's foot, from the top of the stairs to the bottom, with the epithet of a sneaking country put, that did not know when he was used well."[1]

[1] King, *The Frauds of London Detected*, 1770, pp. 16-18. Through

Regarding the conditions under which brothel inmates worked, the money they earned, and the methods employed in securing fresh recruits, William Logan has some revealing statements to make. The mistress of the brothel claimed half a girl's earnings, whether paid in actual fees or in the form of presents; in addition, each inmate was charged £1 a week for board, and she had to buy her own clothes or pay for the loan of them. "A woman who lost her arms in a factory," says Logan, "kept a bad house, and I have seen her standing at the Leeds and Selby railway when the trains came in, for the purpose of entrapping young females from the country. When she did not need them herself, they were sent off to a first- or second-class house, and she received so much money for the 'fresh girls.' "[1]

It was a common practice for the brothel-keepers upon receiving a new, young and particularly alluring recruit, to address letters to gentlemen whose names and addresses were obtained from the *Court Guide*. The communications were sent through the penny post. "I have in my possession," says Talbot, "several of these letters, which have been handed to me by the gentlemen to whom they were addressed. One person, a Frenchwoman, had the effrontery to place on her card, 'opposite Marlborough House.' "[2]

In 1841, states a report of the Chief Commissioner of Police, there were known to be no fewer than 3,325 brothels[3] in the

the centuries prostitutes' bullies display little variation in technique. The methods employed by the pimp even today might be similar to those described by King.

[1] William Logan, *An Exposure from Personal Observations of Female Prostitution in London*, &c.; second edition, Glasgow, 1843, p. 14.

[2] James Beard Talbot, *The Miseries of Prostitution*, London, 1844.

[3] It should be noted that the word *brothel* in connection with this report was used in a police sense, and included houses in which prostitutes were kept, houses in which prostitutes lodged and houses to which prostitutes resorted. The number of establishments in which girls were kept for the purpose of prostitution was compara-

Metropolitan District of London alone. Sir Arthur de Capel Brook, in a report drawn up in 1835, asserted that the total number of improper houses in Lambeth was 1,176, and the number of known prostitutes 2,033; while the Rev. Mr Hughes, of Bedford Chapel, Bloomsbury, stated "that on a space of ground about 700 yards in circumference (St Giles's Rookery) there were 24 houses of ill-fame, containing an average of ten prostitutes to each house." The Rev. Mr Ainsley, one of the secretaries of the City Mission, said "that in the neighbourhood of New Court, there were 22 houses of ill-fame, inhabited by 150 women, besides children."[1]

In those days many of the poorer members of society lived, whether from necessity or choice, among dirt and squalor, bringing up their children in an environment which favoured vice and immorality. It would have been something to marvel at if they had graduated into anything other than petty thieves and prostitutes. For crime and prostitution go hand in hand. As regards the period to which the foregoing remarks apply, that is, the early decades of the nineteenth century, the Report of a Statistical Committee at Leeds, quoted by Talbot, gives an account of the deplorable state of that northern city. "There are 37 houses of ill-fame in one ward, 3 of which are dens of the most infamous description. It is said that in the Boot and Shoe Yard, there are 34 houses containing 57 rooms, each containing an average of 6 persons. In another ward there are several horrible places utterly impassable from filth of the most offensive description." Speaking of Glasgow, the Assistant Commissioner, in his report on the hand-loom weavers, said: "In the lower lodging houses, 10, 12 and sometimes 20 persons, of both sexes and of all ages, sleep promiscuously on

tively small, constituting 410 out of the total number of brothels cited in the report, i.e. 3,325.

[1] For these details I am indebted to the pamphlet entitled *The Miseries of Prostitution*, by James Beard Talbot.

the floor, in different degrees of nakedness. These places are generally, as regards dirt, damp, and decay, such as no person of common humanity would stable a horse in. The lower parts of some dilapidated, dangerous, and condemned houses are either spirit-shops, pawnshops, or eating-houses. Many of the younger girls (and there are a multitude of them) who frequent these places appear to have been driven there by sheer want, and apply to Captain Miller (Chief of the Glasgow Police), in great numbers, to be rescued from misery. No efficient aid can be afforded them under the existing institutions, and hundreds in a year become inured to crime and pass through the rapid career of prostitution, drunkenness, and disease, to an early grave." By a return, furnished to Captain Miller, of visits made to certain rooms situate in the New and Old Wynd, Glasgow, it appears "that on the night of the 4th and 5th September, 1840, there were in one room, 16½ ft. by 10 ft., fourteen prostitutes; and in eleven other rooms, varying from 9 to 14 ft. by 7 to 11 ft., there were 84 prostitutes besides children. There was no furniture in any of these rooms; the poor creatures sleeping only upon shavings."

Mr Talbot made his own personal inquiries, too. In regard to conditions in London, he writes: "I have myself had occasion to visit, lately, the Almonry, Westminster, a limited spot near the Abbey, and abutting upon Tothill-street. I went into a great number of rooms, from the cellar to the attic, and found in each numbers of unfortunate women, varying from four to ten in each apartment; from inquiries made of the police, I learned that almost all the houses were occupied by thieves, receivers of stolen property, and lewd females. Although I did not count the number, I have no hesitation in stating my belief, that it fully equalled, if not exceeded, the [estimate given in the] statement made by Mr Hughes. I have also visited that notorious scene of iniquity, the Mint, situate in the Borough, and, if possible, witnessed a more horrible state of profligacy and crime than that presented in the Almonry. The lowest class of characters assemble here. The houses are filled with mendicant lodgers and prostitutes. In the public-houses, in addition to drinking and all kinds of impurity, dog fighting, badger baiting, and other cruel and barbarous sports are to be seen. The youthful thieves of the metropolis are here trained to become adepts, and the most abominable wickedness prevails. Within the last three weeks, a district, abutting on the Commercial Road, including only four streets, has come under my observation. In these four streets, there are, at the present time, 65 brothels inhabited by 194 females, in all of which the most dreadful scenes are to be witnessed. I might mention other neighbourhoods I have visited, in all of which the same scenes are to be witnessed. I will content myself, however, by mentioning one more circumstance: I recently visited York-square, in the vicinity of Regent's Park, in company with one of the secretaries of the City Mission. All the houses, with the exception of four, were occupied by females following a life of prostitution. I think about 34 were thus tenanted: supposing each house to contain 5 females, which, I have no doubt, is under the actual number, then, in that one square alone, there would be found 170 prostitutes, besides children."[1]

In relation to other cities, this same authority gives the following figures concerning brothels existing at the time of which he was writing (1844): Dublin, 355; Edinburgh, 219; Liverpool, 770; Manchester, 308; Birmingham, 797; Hull, 175; and Norwich, 194. As regards the last-named city, he quotes from the *Norfolk Chronicle* (December 2, 1843) thus: "This city abounds with facilities for the perpetration of robberies. There are not less than 600 taverns and alehouses, besides beershops, in Norwich and its suburbs. It is well known that half of these houses are of the lowest kind, open

[1] J. B. Talbot, *The Miseries of Prostitution*, pp. 23-4.

brothels, resorts of thieves and prostitutes, where robberies are planned, property secreted, and every means afforded for evading justice." Referring to Leeds, William Logan says that in 1840, when the city had a population of 160,000, there were 175 brothels, to each of which were attached an average of four prostitutes. The average number of visits per house was 80 a week, totalling 14,000 visits in all. The average earnings of these 700 prostitutes was thirty shillings a week.

In all these cities at that time the houses of prostitution were classifiable under three heads: (a) regular brothels; (b) dress houses and (c) accommodation houses. The true brothel contained a number of girls, usually varying from ten to twelve, who were in receipt of a regular salary or were paid a portion of the profits. In the dress houses, on the other hand, the inmates received neither salary nor fee: they were fed, clothed and given a place to sleep, and that was all. They did not receive their clients in the houses, but had to seek them outside in the manner of the true street-walker. Says Acton: "The rouged and whitewashed creatures, with painted lips and eyebrows, and false hair, accustomed to haunt Langham Place, portions of the New Road, the Quadrant, the Peristyle of the Haymarket Theatre, the City Road, and the purlieus of the Lyceum, were the most prominent gangs of this description in London. They were watched by persons of their own sex, employed purposely to prevent their abstraction of the lodging-house finery, and clandestine traffic with men. These wretched women, virtually slaves, though nominally free, with bodies and time no longer their own, were restricted, for the convenience of the real proprietors, to certain parades or beats, and from year's end to year's end might be observed on the same side of one particular street, and within a few hundred yards or less of one particular spot. If their solicitations proved unsuccessful, their exertions were stimulated by the proprietor in person, who would sally forth from her den to aid the canvas, to admonish and to swear; and sometimes by the sentinel in charge, who assumed for the time being these functions of authority."[1]

The following account, which presents a picture of the revolting conditions prevalent inside one of the houses of prostitution, is given by Talbot: "A young female, named M——— J———, the daughter of a schoolmaster (now dead), was on Saturday, June 15, 1844, tried at the Central Criminal Court, for robbery. It appeared that, about eight or nine months since, the mother was compelled to take a situation at Dunstable, leaving her daughter with a friend in London, occasionally sending up money for her support. About three weeks since, she was seduced into a brothel in John's-place, Storer-street, Stepney. She was urged to go into the streets by the brothel-keeper, but refused. She was then placed at the door, to invite men into the house. Not having sufficient clothes, some were lent her by the mistress. At length, being ill-used and half-starved, and being disgusted with her course of life, she ran away, taking with her the clothes belonging to the brothel-keeper. A few days after she was given in charge by the keeper of the brothel, who met her in the street, and was committed to Newgate for stealing the clothes.[2] She was very badly diseased. During the time she was in the brothel, all the money she obtained was taken possession of by the brothel-keeper. She was acquitted."

Accommodation houses had no girl inmates, but prostitutes walking the streets could take their clients there, and similarly men were in the habit of taking girls to such places.

A mid-nineteenth-century brothel of the type existing in the East End of London is described by Acton, thus: "The

---

[1] William Acton, *Prostitution considered in its Moral, Social, and Sanitary Aspects*, second edition, 1870, p. 10.

[2] Later on, the law allowed a girl to take clothes in order to escape from a brothel without being liable to prosecution for stealing them.

first house we entered was one in which prostitutes reside. It was kept by a dark, swarthy, crisp-haired Jewess, half creole in appearance, who stated that she was a widow, and that having married a Christian, she had been discarded by her own people. . . . We went upstairs, and saw the rooms, eight in number, which were let out to as many women. The landlady told us that they pay 2s. when they bring home a visitor, and she thought that on an average they are lucky when they bring two each in the course of the evening. This woman was clearly indisposed to let us into her secrets, seeing us accompanied by the Inspectors, and entered into a rambling statement as to the care and leniency with which she treated her lodgers when they were 'out of luck.' She asserted, and the statement was corroborated by the girls, that they kept themselves; two may chum, or sleep together, when disengaged; but they receive the money they earn and are not farmed out. The utmost pressure put upon them is, perhaps, that they are induced to go out and persevere in prostitution when otherwise indisposed to do so. When ill, they apply to the hospital, and St Bartholomew's appeared to be the favourite establishment. This house may be taken as a fair sample of the brothels existing in the East End of London."[1]

Very different were the conditions prevalent in the fashionable West End during the same period. The better-class girls frequented the casinos, notably the Argyll Rooms. For a description of this notorious resort I am again indebted to Acton: "The visitor, on passing the doors, finds himself in a spacious room, the fittings of which are of the most costly description, while brilliant gas illuminations, reflected by numerous mirrors, impart a fairy-like aspect to the scene. . . . The women are of course all prostitutes. They are for the most part pretty, and quietly though expensively dressed, while delicate complexions, unaccompanied by the pallor of ill-health, are

[1] William Acton, *op. cit.*, pp. 22-3.

neither few nor far between. This appearance is doubtless due in many cases to the artistic manner of the makeup by powder and cosmetics, on the employment of which extreme care is bestowed.... Their behaviour is usually quiet, little solicitation is observable, and all the outward proprieties of demeanour and gesture are strictly observed. ... The sum expected by one of these women in return for her favours is about two or three sovereigns. Many will expect those who desire their company to stand them refreshment without stint, not only at the casino, but at some house of call later on in the night, suggesting champagne or 'phiz' as agreeable to their palate, and will be indisposed to return home until they have had their full evening's amusement."[1]

In addition to these recognised types of brothel, public-houses and low-class lodging houses were commonly used by prostitutes. Talbot goes so far as to say that in the ports almost every public-house was a brothel. He writes: "I recently visited Chatham and Sheerness, and found unfortunate women, and sailors and soldiers, congregated in the long rooms attached to public-houses, and was informed that the main dependence of the publican was from these poor deluded creatures. Lieutenants Rivers and Montmorency, of Greenwich Hospital, assured me that it was the common and ordinary usage for loose women to be admitted on board ships of war while coming into port, when in port, and when leaving port, and that they had actually seen more unfortunate females on board than there were men."[2]

Possibly the most sordid of all the prostitutes were those who were patronised by the soldiers. The revelations connected with England's one-time attempt to bring prostitutes living in the garrison towns under police regulation and med-

---

[1] William Acton, *op. cit.*, pp. 19-20.
[2] J. B. Talbot, *The Miseries of Prostitution*, p. 14.

ical inspection indicated a sorry state of affairs.[1] Even sorrier, however were the conditions under which lived many of the "camp followers." One particularly notorious gathering of these women was near Kildare, in Ireland. The story of this community of "bushwomen," as revealed in an anonymous pamphlet entitled *The Wren of the Curragh*, is a terrible one. The conditions under which these girls and young women (mostly between the ages of seventeen and twenty-five years), around sixty in number, existed were pitiable where they were not disgusting. Their habitations or "nests" were constructed of tree branches or furze; each had an interior space of about 9 ft. long by 7 ft. broad, and the roof was no more than 4½ ft. from the ground. They had the appearance of huge rudely shaped birds' nests, hence the name. Unwittingly, these women were, it would appear, experimenting in communism, for according to the author of the pamphlet: "What each company get is thrown into a common purse, and the nest is provisioned out of it. The ruling principle evidently is to share each other's fortunes and misfortunes." All the evidence available, however, supports the idea that misfortune was the ruling note. For the deplorable conditions under which they existed told their tale. "There was a common look, shocking to see, of hard depravity—the look of hopeless, miserable, but determined and defiant wickedness. Fine faces, and young ones too, were marred into something quite terrible by this look, and the spirit of it seemed to move in the lazy swing of their limbs, and was certainly heard in their voices. And lastly they are dressed alike. All day they lounge in a half-naked state, clothed simply in the one frieze petticoat, and another equally foul cast loosely over their shoulders, though towards evening they put on decent attire."[2] Their conduct was atrocious, displaying the utmost depths of shamelessness

[1] See pages 132-4.
[2] *The Wren of the Curragh*, p. 25.

and licentiousness. Practically every night they sallied forth
to engage in drunken orgies. But let me reproduce here, in the
author's own words, a description of what he heard and witnessed on that ever-to-be-remembered night when, in the
course of his investigations, he visited one of these "nests."

"Presently the sound of distant voices was heard; it came
nearer and nearer, and its shrillness and confusion made it
known to me that it was indeed a party of returning wrens
—far from sober. They were, in fact, mad drunk; and the
sound of their voices as they came on through the dense
darkness, screaming obscene songs, broken by bursts of
horrible laughter, with now and then a rattling volley of
oaths which told that fighting was going on, was staggering.
I confess I now felt uncomfortable. I had only seen the
wren sober, or getting sober; what she might be in *that*
raging state of drunkenness I had yet to find out; and the
discovery threatened to be very unpleasant. The noise came
nearer, and was more shocking because you could disen-
tangle the voices and track each through its own course
of swearing, or of obscene singing and shouting, or
of dreadful threats which dealt in detail with every part
of the human frame. 'Is this your lot?' I asked my companion, with some apprehension, as at length the shameful
crew burst out of the darkness. 'Some ov 'em, I think.' But
no, they passed on; such a spectacle as made me tremble.
I felt like a man respited when the last woman went staggering by. Again voices were heard, this time proceeding from
the women belonging to the bush where I was spending so
uncomfortable an evening. Five in all, two tipsy and three
comparatively sober, they soon presented themselves at the
door. One of them was Billy's mother. At the sound of her
voice the child woke up and cried for her. She was the most
forbidding-looking creature in the whole place; but she

hastened to divest herself, outside, of her crinoline and the rest of her walking attire (nearly all she had on), and came in and nursed the boy very tenderly. The other wrens also took off gown and petticoat, and folding them up made seats of them within the nest. Then came the important inquiry from the watching wren: 'What luck have you had?'—to which the answer was: 'Middling.' Without the least scruple they counted up what they had got among them—a poor account: it was enough to make a man's heart bleed to hear the details and to see the actual money."[1]

Glancing at the conditions of prostitution in London during the eighties, as depicted in the expository pages of *The Pall Mall Gazette,* it is noteworthy that, with the passing of years, basically there is for the finding little change, and certainly none for the better. These revelatory articles disclosed a dreadful state of affairs. They disclosed, among other things, that owing to the demand at high prices for virgins the traffickers were induced to go to great lengths and to display much ingenuity in enticing young girls to sell their bodies. Admittedly in most cases every effort was made to secure those who were willing to make the sacrifice; but in very many cases, as was abundantly evident, the loss of virginity was brought about by deliberate misrepresentation, and in circumstances virtually indistinguishable from rape. Apropos of this, from *The Pall Mall Gazette* itself I cull the following:

"In the course of my investigations I heard some strange tales concerning the precautions taken to render escape impossible for the girl whose ruin, with or without her consent, has been resolved upon. One fact, which is of quite recent occurence in a fashionable London suburb, the

[1] *The Wren of the Curragh,* pp. 49-50.

accuracy of which I was able to verify, is an illustration of the extent to which those engaged in the traffic are willing to go to supply the caprices of their customers. To oblige a wealthy customer ... an eminently respectable lady undertook that whenever the girl was 14 or 15 years of age she should be strapped down hand and foot to the four posts of the bedstead, so that all resistance save that of unavailing screaming would be impossible.... Strapping down for violation used to be common occurrence in Half-moon-street and in Anna Rosenberg's brothel at Liverpool."[1]

In the vast majority of cases the loss of a girl's virginity meant the adoption of prostitution as a career.[2] In some instances a girl who had willingly succumbed to temptation did not dare return to her parents; and it was the same with one who had been induced to place herself in circumstances where she could not escape assault. Here, from the stark pages of *The Pall Mall Gazette,* let me quote the statement of an ex-brothel-keeper: "Did they begin willingly? Some; others had no choice. How had they no choice? Because they never knew anything about it till the gentleman was in their bedroom, and then it was too late. I or my girls would entice fresh girls in, and persuade them to stay out too late till they were locked out, and then a pinch of snuff in their beer would keep them snug until the gentleman had his way." This brothel-keeper told of picking up a girl aged about 13, engaging her as a maid, and taking her to London. "A gentleman paid me £13 for the first of her, soon after she came to town.

[1] From an article entitled "The Maiden Tribute to Modern Babylon," in *The Pall Mall Gazette*, July, 6 1885, p. 6.
[2] In much the same way, an unmarried Spanish mother can even today write off her chances of ever becoming a bride, and is much more likely to become a prostitute.

She was asleep when he did it—sound asleep. To tell the truth, she was drugged. It is often done."[1]

At that time, in the 1880's, the age of consent was 13, and on the streets of London town there were for the finding any number of young prostitutes between the ages of 13 and 16. Previous to 1875, unbelievable as it may seem in these days, the age of consent was 12. And so, in those nineteenth-century days of evil, infants of 12 and 13 years could surrender their virginity if they wished, and there was no means of punishing the man who took advantage of the girl's innocence. In this connection the figures relative to the seduction of these young girls, as presented in *The Pall Mall Gazette,* disclose a truly remarkable and lamentable state of affairs.

"The Rescue Society, of Finsbury-pavement, which has an experience of thirty-one years, has kept for twenty-five years a record of the ages at which those whom they have rescued lost their character. The following are the numbers of the rescued who were seduced at the ages of 12 and 13 for 1862 to 1875, when the close time was raised to thirteen —33, 55, 65, 107, 102, 103, 77, 60, 78, 62, 40, 43, 30: total 855, or 66 per annum between the ages of twelve and thirteen. From 1875 to 1883 the figures were as follows: 22, 24, 19, 20, 16, 14, 15, 10, 7, total 147; average 16 per annum. Allowance must be made for the fact that the total number rescued in 1883 was only half that rescued in 1880, but even then the total number of children seduced at twelve and thirteen would have been reduced by one-half owing to the raising of the age."[2]

In England today there are, of course, no tolerated houses

[1] From an article entitled "The Maiden Tribute to Modern Babylon," in *The Pall Mall Gazette,* July 6, 1885, p. 4.
[2] *Ibid.,* July 8, 1885, p. 2.

of prostitution. The Criminal Law Amendment Act of 1885 did away with this type of brothel altogether.[1] It should however be clearly understood that the absence of brothels does little to lessen the incidence of prostitution. It does not prevent prostitutes carrying on their trade. All they have to do is to live separately instead of congregating in numbers under one roof. To come within the legal definition of a brothel the premises must be used by at least *two* women for the purpose of prostitution.[2]

It is interesting how from time to time the haunts of prostitutes in big cities change. In London in the eighteenth and early nineteenth centuries Covent Garden was well noted. Later the Haymarket and other places were patronised which have in recent decades been quite deserted by prostitutes.[3] For instance, a senior Police Officer mentioned to a Select Committee of the House of Lords in 1881 that "from 3 o'clock in the afternoon it is impossible for any respectable woman to walk from the top of the Haymarket to Wellington Street, Strand. From 3 or 4 o'clock in the afternoon Villiers Street and Charing Cross Station and the Strand are crowded with prostitutes, who are there openly soliciting prostitution in broad daylight. At half-past twelve at night a calculation was made a short time ago that there were 500 prostitutes between Piccadilly Circus and the bottom of Waterloo Place." In that short and previously crowded distance it is very doubtful if one prostitute has solicited during the past twenty years, at least.

---

[1] Even before the passing of this Act there was observable during the nineteenth century a remarkable decline in the number of brothels.

[2] See page 171.

[3] There is a mine of information about Victorian prostitution in the celebrated anonymous erotic autobiography *Walter: My Secret Life*, edited by Drs E. & P. Kronhausen (Polybooks, London, 2 volumes, 9/6d each.)

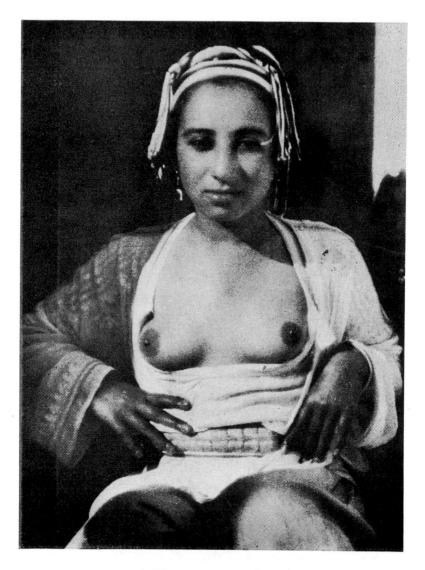

A Moroccan prostitute

Collection Viollet

Japanese courtesans in their cages
From *The Nightless City*

Luxury in a former Paris brothel at 6 rue des Moulins

Collection Romi

The Empire Lounge, Leicester Square, London

From *The Sketch*, 1894

XI: HISTORICAL ASPECTS OF PROSTITUTION IN THE UNITED STATES OF AMERICA

READERS of both fact and fiction dealing with the frontier towns of America are familiar with the "gay ladies" who were to be found in the saloons of every cattle town and mining camp in the West. In those days women of respectability were few where rough men lived, fought and drank. As a result men enormously outnumbered women, and this disproportion of the sexes developed prostitution in a manner and to an extent unknown in other communities that were better balanced. There was little in the way of regulation, the women practising their trade openly and blatantly.

In the cities and towns of the East things were very different, following much the same lines as in Europe: attempts being made continuously and variedly to give the bitter pill of harlotry a more palatable coating. Conditions varied in different States, but apart from occasional attempts at suppression prostitution ranked as a tolerated evil, and in most cities "parlour houses" of some kind or other were there for the finding.

The "parlour house" of America was really a brothel. In the early and middle decades of the nineteenth century the term was virtually restricted to the highest-class houses, where the appointments were luxurious, the girls attractive and magnificently dressed, also as a rule well educated, the

97

clientele select, and the charges exceptionally high. But gradually the custom grew of calling any brothel a "parlour house," and by the commencement of the twentieth century the different classes were designated in accordance with the fees charged, but they were all "parlour houses." Thus there were the ten- or twenty-dollar houses heading the list, and the fifty-cent houses at the tail end.

But whatever the type of house, the principle was the same. Apart from the woman in charge, and the servants, the house was inhabited solely by prostitutes, each of whom had her own private room. All the girls assembled in the parlour at stated times, where the guests congregated. The girls never walked the streets in search of clients. These invariably came to the house and made their choice of partners in the parlour. The proprietors of the brothels attracted clients in many and devious ways: they had agents working on commission, notably porters at hotels, chauffeurs, bartenders and the like, who had exceptional opportunities for contacting likely men. There was a regular medical inspection, generally once a week. The girl received a portion of the fee charged, usually 50 per cent. In some houses the brass check system was used; in others a punched card method was adopted.

In the early days of American civilisation the girls were of American birth, descendants of the first settlers. But as the attractions of the fabulous American Republic became known far and wide and the great trek from Europe started, it was from the ranks of these foreign girls that the *habituées* of the brothels were recruited. Apart from the fact that aliens are always easier to seduce and to "manage" than native-born women, those who make of prostitution a business know well that they are on far safer ground if the victims of the trade are girls of foreign birth or upbringing. These vice merchants are aware of the fact that the government, the societies for suppressing vice and the public generally are much more likely to rise up in anger and demand the cleaning up of the cities if the girls concerned are of home vintage than if they have come from other countries. Moreover, the patrons of the brothels for the most part find foreign girls more attractive than those of their own nationality; this is a truism applying in every country on the face of the globe.

Knowing little English, unacquainted with the ways of the country in which she was living, an alien girl was easy prey for her exploiters. She was charged ridiculously high prices for clothing supplied by the manageress, for medical examination, and for various other items, all of which were entered in the books against her share of the fees earned. The result was that she was perpetually in debt to the management. Additionally, these girls, because of their moronic ingenuousness, coupled with their ignorance of America and its language, were easily intimidated. They knew nothing of the law, and accepted as gospel the assertions made and stressed by the brothel-keepers that any attempt to escape would inevitably lead to their arrest and imprisonment.

These foreign women, in many cases, were deliberately imported for the specific purpose of practising prostitution. Most of them were already engaged in the profession in the countries of their birth, but in some instances, no doubt, they were brought into or induced to enter the American Republic under false pretences, usually by the promise of work of an alluring nature or at high wages. In a report issued in 1909 by the U.S. Immigration Commission, a typical case is given, in which "a French girl seized in a raid on a disorderly house in Chicago stated to the United States authorities that she was approached when she was but fourteen years of age; that her procurer promised her employment in America as a lady's maid or a companion at wages far beyond any that she could ever hope to get in France; that she came with him to the United States, and upon her arrival in Chicago was sold into a house of ill-fame."[1] Sometimes these girls were brought into the country as wives or close relatives of their importers, says the report. "In the case of the Japanese, they often came to join a man to whom, in accordance with the customs of their country, they had been married by proxy."[2]

By no means all the foreign recruits to the brothels were specifically imported, however. The traders in women were quite aware that the stream of immigrants pouring into America from all parts of Europe offered rich pickings. A statement by Edwin W. Sims, United States District Attorney in Chicago, to the aforementioned Commission, is revealing in this respect. He said:

"The hirelings of this traffic are stationed at certain points of entry in Canada where large numbers of immigrants are landed to do what is known in their parlance as 'cutting-out' work. In other words, these watchers for human prey scan the immigrants as they come down the gangplank of a vessel which has just arrived and 'spot' the girls who are unaccompanied by fathers, mothers, brothers or relatives to protect them. The girl who has been spotted as a desirable and unprotected victim is properly approached by a man who speaks her language and is immediately offered employment at good wages, with all expenses to the destination to be paid by the man. Most frequently laundry work is the bait held out, sometimes housework or employment in a candy shop or factory. The object of the negotiations is to 'cut out' the girl from any of her associates and to get her to go with him. Then the only thing is to accomplish her ruin by the shortest route. If she cannot be cajoled or enticed by the promises of an easy

[1] *Report on Importing Women for Immoral Purposes*, Washington, 1909, p. 15.
[2] *Ibid.*, p. 9.

time, plenty of money, fine clothes, and the usual stock of allurements—or a fake marriage—then harsher methods are resorted to. In some instances the hunters really marry their victims. As to the sterner methods, it is, of course, impossible to speak explicitly beyond the statement that intoxication and drugging are often resorted to as a means to reduce the victims to a state of helplessness, and sheer physical violence is a common thing."[1]

The prices paid for attractive girls, according to this same report, were often high. Five hundred dollars was no uncommon sum for a French prostitute delivered in the U.S.A. For an innocent youngster unattached to any pimp, a brothel proprietor would pay even higher. Among the papers seized from the Dufaur house, Chicago, in 1908, was evidence that Dufaur had paid one thousand dollars for an exceptionally attractive girl.[2] Japanese girls were purchased in Seattle for four hundred dollars each. Chinese girls, who were particularly difficult to import because of the Chinese Exclusion Act, were much dearer, bringing from two thousand to three thousand dollars each.[3]

It is true that "parlour houses" or brothels were prohibited in most States, but the law was virtually powerless to prevent their existence. The local authorities for the most part turned a blind eye to the operations of the vice traffickers, and the public, subscribing most firmly to the age-old opinion that without prostitutes respectable women would be continually in danger of being raped, backed up authority with word and deed. In all cases, whether there was toleration or not, a system of bribery ensured a blind-eye attitude on the part of the police.

There was, however, no consistent method of dealing with

[1] *Report on Importing Women for Immoral Purposes*, Washington, 1909, p. 16.   [2] *Ibid.*   [3] *Ibid.*

the problem of prostitution. The only consistent feature was the conviction that the evil must be tolerated. In some cities there was regulation, or rather attempted regulation, which virtually amounted to the attempt to segregate prostitutes by means of an admitted "red-light" district, with a system of medical inspection. In other cities there was no such attempt at segregation or even regulation.

The exploitation of vice reached its apogee around 1870 and continued with little diminution until well into the first decade of the twentieth century. In Chicago, especially, was prostitution particularly rampant during this period. South State Street, South Dearborn Street, and other nearby thoroughfares, bristled with brothels of all types and classes. Writing of Custom House Place (afterwards renamed Federal Street) at the time of the first World Fair to be held in Chicago, Clifton R. Wooldridge, a former detective, says:

"Here at all hours of the day and night women could be seen at the doors and windows, frequently half-clad, making an exhibition of themselves and using vulgar and obscene language.... It was no unusual thing in those days to see from fifty to one hundred women lounging in the doors and windows in this one block at one time. The *habituées* of this place embraced every nationality, both black and white, their ages ranging from eighteen to fifty years.... In these houses could be found every low and demoralizing phase of life that the human mind could think of. Many of these women were even lower than brutes."[1]

Huge profits were made from these brothels, and in particular from the more expensive and elaborate establishments. The

[1] Quoted by Herbert Asbury in his book *The Underworld of Chicago*, from *Hands Up! In the World of Crime, or Twelve Years a Detective*, by Clifton R. Wooldridge, Chicago, 1906.

rococo and extravagantly appointed house in South Clark Street, run by the notorious Carrie Watson, is said to have provided her with a princely income, and enabled her to retire, after a quarter of a century, an extremely wealthy woman. Then there was the South Dearborn Street brothel, built by Christopher Columbus Crabb and Lizzie Allen, which later, when owned and run by the famous Everleigh sisters and known as the Everleigh Club, was to acquire world-wide renown as "the most notorious, the most luxurious, and at the same time the most consistently profitable bordello that the United States, and probably the rest of the world as well, has ever seen."[1] Another eminently successful female operator was Vina Fields, who, says Herbert Asbury, had the largest brothel of her day. Also, according to the same authority, although a strict disciplinarian, she treated her girls extremely well, giving them "a larger percentage of their earnings than any other madame in Chicago."[2]

Apart from the brothels, there were the saloons in which professional girls picked up clients and to which they took men whom they had solicited on the streets. Most notorious of these were the "Raines Law" hotels, which were little better than disorderly houses.[3] Any saloon, restaurant or similar establishment with a minimum of ten bedrooms available for lodgers could be called a hotel and was permitted to sell

[1] Herbert Asbury, *The Underworld of Chicago*, Robert Hale, London, 1941, p. 243. This important and interesting work, to which I am indebted for these details concerning the Chicago brothels, deals exhaustively with prostitution in Chicago, constituting a valuable and profound study of the city's underworld.

[2] *Ibid.*, p. 141.

[3] A disorderly house, in the United States of America, is one which violates section 1146 of the Penal law. The admission of one woman on two occasions in a single night accompanied by two different men; the letting of the same room to two different couples in one night, or the admission of women who are known to be habitual prostitutes constitute such violation of the law.

alcoholic drinks on Sundays. Many of these saloons were patronised by prostitutes.

Gradually, however, changes came over the scene. In one way or another the public were rebelling against vice in, at any rate, its more blatant forms. Sensational accounts, some true and many apocryphal, respecting the so-called "white-slave" traffic led to the passing of the notorious Mann Act. This Act, which became law in 1910, was intended to prevent the transportation of girls by vice traffickers from one part of the country to another. In accordance with its provisions the act of taking a female into another State for the purpose of fornication is a criminal offence, punishable by fine or imprisonment, and the maximum penalties are heavy. The question of whether the woman goes voluntarily or is transported against her will does not affect the matter. The Act is not without its evils, and it has been bitterly criticised. For although, true enough, it is rarely invoked to deal with cases of immorality obviously unconnected with "white slavery," the possibility of the Act being interpreted so as to include ordinary cases of fornication committed after travelling to another State, by two persons who are not husband and wife, cannot be ruled out. It often leads to blackmail, and the fact that the woman concerned cannot be prosecuted enhances considerably the manner in which the Act can be used for this purpose.

A more serious blow to the vice traffickers however was the passing, in 1919, of the Volstead Act, which brought about the closing of the saloons and other drinking establishments that had largely taken the place of the old "parlour houses." Similarly the street-walkers, badgered by the police to an extent that made their profession a game of hide and seek, were reduced in numbers almost to the point of extinction, the few that remained having to exercise the greatest vigilance or to pay heavy "graft" in order to keep out of the clutches of authority.

All of which does not mean that fornication showed the slightest sign of diminution. On the contrary, if anything, extra-marital intercourse and perverse forms of sexual vice showed a sharp increase. Immorality took on different aspects, that was all.

In addition to the factors already mentioned, the early decades of the twentieth century were marked by the emancipation of women on a scale hitherto unknown and undreamed of, and the coincident increase in knowledge of and facilities for the practice of birth control. The anxiety to safeguard her virginity and the reputed sexual anaesthesia of a woman in the past had been largely conditioned, whether or not the point was conceded, by her liability to present evidence of her frailty in the shape of an unwanted pregnancy. The advancement in contraceptive technique, the wider knowledge concerning this technique, and, especially, the increased confidence in its efficiency, removed, so far as a large and constantly growing section of the female population were concerned, the fear connected with any departures from the strait and narrow path. The consequence of all this, coupled with the before-mentioned emancipation of woman, was that girls of respectability were more and more inclined to embark upon sexual adventure of a type previously restricted to servant girls, morons and others who could be inveigled into such experiments. As a result the professional prostitute had to meet competition of a new and disturbing kind. For the first time in history the girl of respectability, in the form of the "gold-digger" on the one hand and the "good-time girl" on the other, encroached to a perilous extent on the prostitute's preserves. While fornication increased, the number of professional girls decreased. This was the paradox of twentieth-century vice.

To some extent the repeal of prohibition reintroduced the use of saloons by prostitutes, but not to any degree comparable to the early days of the century. The night clubs and dance halls which became the rendezvous of vice during the days of prohibition remained the main resorts of all but the lowest classes of professional women. In many cases, too, these night clubs and dance halls, as well as roadhouses, cafés, tea-rooms, massage establishments and the rest, were merely places where the preliminaries were settled and meetings arranged for a later date.

The old "red-light" district, which was a feature of so many American cities, is now virtually non-existent, for brothels in the real sense of the word are prohibited in almost every State. Prostitutes there are, and in large numbers, of course. The methods of keeping their activities in check and at the same time tolerating prostitution as a necessary evil are on much the same lines as in England, most States having laws which enable the common prostitute to be prosecuted for disorderly conduct or vagrancy. The rigour with which the campaign against prostitution in many American cities is waged ebbs and flows. There are periodical clean-ups, during which prostitutes and all those engaged in the business of vice are proceeded against to the point of persecution, followed by long periods of inactivity by the moralistic associations, during which the vice traffickers once more become active.

The fact that organised vice at any time and at all times is a lucrative business causes the controllers of the gangs to exercise additional care in the methods they employ, to spend more money in procuring "protection". Behind the prostitute in so many cases looms the sinister figure of the pimp, who often enough is the agent of a powerful ring of traffickers. He it is who makes the necessary arrangements with the police whereby they pursue a policy of non-interference; and while today there seems little likelihood of any return to the conditions which at one time were to be found in the vice districts of New York, Chicago, St Louis, New Orleans, San Francisco and other big cities, there are still for the finding plenty of night-spots which are camouflaged brothels or assignation houses. The pimp of today is all the more dangerous because he is, as often as not, educated as well as sophisticated; the present-day prostitute, whether professional or amateur, is, generally speaking, far removed in bearing, manners and appearance from her prototype of years ago, and in many respects she, too, has increased potentialities for evil.

Today the position in the U.S.A. is that in many States prostitution is an offence in itself; in a few soliciting is punishable; in nearly all there are special provisions regarding the compulsory treatment of professional women suffering from venereal disease, and houses of prostitution are prohibited.

XII: HISTORICAL ASPECTS OF PROSTITUTION IN ORIENTAL COUNTRIES

ALMOST a century ago, Francis L. Hawks penned the following significant words: "There is one feature in the society of Japan by which the superiority of the people, to all other Oriental nations, is clearly manifest. Woman is recognised as a companion, and not merely treated as a slave. That in the large towns and cities of Japan there is great licentiousness it is reasonable to suppose, for such seems, unhappily, a universal law in all great communities; but it must be said to the credit of the Japanese women, that during all the time of the presence of the squadron in the bay of Yedo, there was none of the usual indication of wantonness and license on the part of the female sex in their occasional relations with the miscellaneous ships' people."[1]

The companionate attitude towards women generally, to which Hawks refers, was extended towards that section of the female population which, in so many other countries, was ostracised. Indeed, in no other country on the face of the earth has the woman of easy virtue received the respect accorded her in Japan. For the Japanese, believing, like Europeans and Americans, that the prostitute has an essential place in civilised life, have carried this belief to its logical conclusion,

[1] Francis L. Hawks, *Narrative of the Expedition of an American Squadron to the China Seas and Japan*, 1856, p. 462.

refusing to ostracise any female who is filling what is admitted to be so important a role in the life of the community. As a result of this attitude on the part of the government and the public, it has been customary for a Japanese girl to engage in prostitution as she engaged in any other kind of work. To her it has always represented a means of earning money. And because of this outlook, in Japan there are perhaps more *temporary* prostitutes than in any other country in the world. For the fact of being or of having been a prostitute has never been a bar to the securing of some other kind of work, to making a satisfactory marriage, or to returning home. Until recent years, and before their prohibition, even the brothels were no hole-and-corner affairs; on the contrary they had the appearance "of wealthy and respectable Japanese hotels."[1] Men did not sneak into them as if they were fearful of being seen entering a den of iniquity, but went there as openly as they would to a restaurant or a theatre. Apropos of this outlook on the part of respectable men, Johns says: "I have called on a Japanese business man at his office and been told that he was at the brothel, and if I wished to call there I should be able to see him."[2]

For many centuries an organised system of prostitution prevailed in Japan, there being references by Oye Tadafusa and other historians to such a system being existent in ancient times. It seems to have been usual to restrict the brothels to certain specific parts of a city. In relation to this practice Kaempfer mentions that in Nagasaki, during the seventeenth century, the houses of prostitution were all in one part of the city, comprising two streets. According to this historian "the girls are purchased when very young, from their parents. The price varies in proportion to their beauty and the number of years agreed for, which is, generally speaking, ten or twenty,

---

[1] Leslie W. Johns, *Japan, Reminiscences and Realities*, Stanley Paul, London, n.d., p. 134. [2] *Ibid.*

more or less. Every bawd keeps as many as he is able, in one house together, from seven to thirty. They are very commodiously lodged in handsome apartments and great care is taken to teach them to dance, sing, play upon musical instruments, to write letters and in all other respects to qualify them for the way of life they are obliged to lead. The old ones, being more skilful and expert, instruct the young ones, and these in their turn serve them as their mistresses. Those who make considerable improvements in what they are taught, and for their beauty, and agreeable behaviour, are oftener sent for, to the great advantage of their masters, are also by him better accommodated in clothes and lodging, all at the expense of their lovers, who must pay so much the dearer for their favours. The price paid to their landlord is from one *maas* to two *itzebi* for a night, beyond which they are forbidden to ask, under severe penalties. One of the sorriest, and almost worn by too much use, must watch the house overnight, in a small room adjoining the door, where any passenger may have to do with her, paying but one *maas*. Others are sentenced to keep watch by way of a punishment for their misbehaviour. After having served their time, if they are married they pass among the common people for honest women."[1]

The priests, states this same authority, encouraged prostitution, and many of the temples were little better than brothels. Humbert mentions the practice at one time of exhibiting in some of the temples portraits of famous courtesans, much in the way that portraits of actresses and film stars are exhibited in theatres and cinemas today.

In the tea houses, which have always been a feature of Japanese life, were to be found, at the time of which Kaempfer writes, numerous attractive girls who were, in reality, prostitutes. They engaged openly and brazenly in solicitation. At the wayside inns the same thing happened. It was the custom of

[1] E. Kaempfer, *History of Japan*, 1727.

these girls, after dressing in their most alluring clothes and making free and skilful use of cosmetics, to stand at the door of the inn or tea room, or seat themselves on a bench nearby, and accost with smiles and witticisms those males who entered or even passed by. Where there happened to be two of these inns near each other the rivalry displayed by these girls was keen indeed. Such competition was particularly fierce in the villages of Akasaki and Goy, which, says Kaempfer, "are particularly famous on this account, all the houses therein being so many inns, or rather bawdy houses, each furnished with no fewer than three, six or seven of these wenches, for which reason also they are called the great storehouse of Japanese whores, and by way of banter the common grind mill. Very seldom do any Japanese pass through the villages but they pick up some of these whores and have to do with them. There is hardly a public inn upon the great island of Nippon but what may not be called a bawdy house, and if there be too many customers resort to one place, the neighbouring innkeepers will friendly like and willingly lend their own wenches, on condition that what money they get shall be faithfully paid them. Nor is it a new custom come up lately. On the contrary, it is of very old date, and took its rise many hundred years ago in the time of General and first secular monarch Joritomo, who, apprehensive lest his soldiers weary of his long and tedious expedition, and desiring to return home to their wives and children, should desert his army, thought it much more advisable to indulge them in this particular, and to gratify their carnal appetites by allowing public and private bawdy houses."[1]

It was in the tea houses or *hikite-jaya* that negotiations often took place between prostitutes and their clients: the attendants arranging matters. From a late nineteenth-century description of these rendezvous we learn that on the arrival

[1] E. Kaempfer, *History of Japan*, 1727.

of a visitor one of the attendants, or sometimes the proprietress herself, greeted him warmly at the door, took him inside and asked him which particular brothel he had in mind, and, should he be acquainted with the ladies attached to it, the name of any particular girl he would prefer to meet. These points being decided upon, the attendant escorted him to the brothel, where she carried out the necessary negotiations, after which she waited upon the visitor during the banquet which was an essential part of the ceremonial procedure, and finally conducted him to his sleeping apartment, where she waited until his "lady friend" arrived, and then discreetly slipped away.[1]

Some of these prostitutes had no voice whatever in the choice of their profession: they had been purchased from their parents in infancy by the brothel-owners and educated and trained for their calling. Others had sold themselves for a specific period. In Mayhew's well-known study of prostitution we read: "Some parents apprentice out their daughters for a term of years to this abominable profession, and the girls then return to honourable life. The houses they frequent continually resound with music. At Jeddo, a traveller was informed, there was one brothel, or rather temple of prostitution, where 600 women were maintained. Notwithstanding this number, young men were nightly refused admittance, from the overcrowded state of the rooms. Passing through the streets of the brothel-quarter, Golovnin saw groups of girls standing about the doors; some of them were in the bloom of youth, and so handsome that they appeared fascinating even to the European eye."[2]

[1] For additional information respecting these *hikite-jaya*, or "introducing tea houses", the reader is referred to that interesting and unique book *The Nightless City* (pp. 40-54), to which I am indebted for these details.

[2] Henry Mayhew, *London Labour and the London Poor*, Griffin, Bohn & Co., London, 1862, p. 139.

When voluntary recruitment failed, the unscrupulous owners of the brothels employed *zegen* to obtain girls, and these *zegen*, who were prepared to go to any lengths to secure what they wanted, in turn sent their agents into the remote country districts with instructions to procure recruits by one means or another: to buy, beg, borrow or steal. They brought back young girls whom they locked up securely till the moment for their transfer to the brothel-keepers. "How they maltreated the poor wretches whom they had kidnapped," writes the author of *The Nightless City*, "may be inferred from the fact that the owners of these 'registry offices' were in the habit of stripping the girls absolutely naked every night, and hiding their clothes under their own mattress lest the unhappy victims should escape. When the women were about to be sold to the brothels, with whom the men had made previous arrangements, they were nicely dressed in hired clothes (in order to make them appear to better advantage and thus enhance their selling price) and taken round as 'goods on view.' Then followed protracted negotiations between the parties interested, each haggling over the bargain like a fishmonger and a housewife, the *zegen* trying to squeeze out as much money as possible from the intending buyers, and the brothel-keeper endeavouring to beat him down."[1]

Various efforts were made to bring to an end the activities of these agents, including, in 1792, the prohibition of the selling of women; but the practice continued in some form or other until 1872. In that year the Japanese government issued a decree (Number 295) which contained a clause reading: "The release of all prostitutes, singing girls, and other persons bound to serve for any term of years, is hereby ordered, and it is further directed that no suits relating to debts incurred by, or on account of such persons, shall be entertained."

The law restricting brothels to specific parts of the cities

[1] *The Nightless City*, pp. 129-130.

was brought into force at the beginning of the seventeenth century, apparently the first city in which such an arrangement was enforced being Yedo. The person responsible was a man named Shoji Jinyemon, who not only formulated the scheme but was appointed the first director of the prostitute quarter in the city of Yedo. It was in this way that was born the notorious Yoshiwara, or brothel quarter. Each city had its Yoshiwara, which was in actual fact the prototype of the "red-light" district of an American town.

The Yoshiwara did, however, boast certain characteristics not to be found in the brothels of Europe and America. The girls, in the better-class houses at any rate, showed a superiority over the brothel inmates of other countries, while the method of getting acquainted and the preliminary conversation lacked much of the sordidness and business-like manner usual in the Western world. But the main and most notoriously distinctive feature was the exhibition of the prostitutes in "cages." By the size and embellishment of these "cages" were indicated the class of brothel to which the inmates were attached. In the early days of the practice there were five classes of brothels. The girls belonging to the cheapest type were displayed in "cages" which were so low that the inmates were obliged to lie down; while elaborate high "cages" with widely spaced bars housed the girls from the better-class brothels. From the year 1872 the number of classes into which brothels were divided was reduced to three, the most exclusive and expensive houses dispensing with "cages" altogether, clients having to make their overtures through one of the attendants at a tea house.

It must not for a moment be supposed that the girls "lived" in their "cages," or indeed that the majority spent anything more than comparatively brief periods in them. During the day, at any rate, the "cages" were empty. It was when darkness was beginning to fall that the brothel-ladies, powdered and painted, trooped into their respective "cages," where each one remained until some onlooker fell a victim to her charms, or until it became apparent that there was to be no business that particular night.

Writing in 1899, before the prohibition of these "cages," the author of *The Nightless City* sagely points out that the main objection "to the public exhibition of handsomely dressed women is that it tempts youths who might otherwise remain chaste, and attracts them to the brothel-quarters." For although no one, whether youth or adult, need have visited the Yoshiwara, human nature being what it is few boys and young men failed to gaze upon these attractive girls. The prohibition of the system, continues this writer, "will mean that men will be obliged to enter the houses in cold blood for a definite purpose, and not be exposed to the temptation of being drawn in by the sight of a pretty face exposed as 'on sale.' "[1]

The living accommodation of a prostitute depended upon the class to which she belonged, and the money she was in a position to pay the brothel-owner for accommodation. The usual run of prostitute had two apartments, one being a living room and the other a reception room. Some of the higher-class girls, the "stars" of the Yoshiwara, had three rooms. On the other hand, the lowest type of prostitute had no separate living room at all, sharing with others a common apartment, and having the use of one of a number of small rooms when she succeeded in attracting a client. And, affirms the anonymous author of *Notes on the History of the Yoshiwara of Yedo,* there were some of the very lowest brothels where the girls and their guests "slept together in a single room."

According to the author of *The Nightless City,* prostitutes of the highest class wore the most costly clothing and had their own personal attendants. This writer quotes a descrip-

[1] *The Nightless City,* p. 285.

tion from the pen of a novelist relating to a prostitute of this class, thus:

"The gorgeousness of her wearing apparel almost defies description. Her dress consists of a long robe of richly embroidered silk brocade. Her head is ornamented by a dazzling glory of hair-pins (made of the finest tortoise shell) which glitter around her head like the lambent aureole of a saint, while her ravishing beauty is such that the mere sight of her face will steal away one's very soul. ... From this description, the neatness of her apartments, the tasteful arrangement of her furniture and the dainty elegance of her personal effects may well be imagined."[1]

From time to time regulations relating to the dress of prostitutes were issued by the authorities, and in this way periods of simplicity followed those of luxuriance. Early in the nineteenth century "the zenith of barbaric splendour was attained. Costumes of crêpe, velvet, figured satin, plain satin, *habutae,* etc., were freely used, while *obi* (sashes) were made of velvet, gold-brocade, silk-brocade, damask, etc. As to colours and patterns, these were chosen according to the taste of the individual courtesan and were by no means uniform."[2] At that time no prostitute was allowed "to wear a dress unsuitable to her particular rank in the brothel, even though she could afford it, but nowadays the girls are at liberty to wear any clothes they choose and can pay for, especially if they are popular and beautiful women."[3] The already mentioned delicateness of approach and the ceremonial overtures that were necessary preliminaries were particularly marked where these queens of the Yoshiwara were concerned.

[1] *The Nightless City,* pp. 71-2. The extract is from *Kōshoku-Shōgyō-Shokoku-Monogatari,* by Shōzan (pseudonym of the well-known novelist Kyōden).
[2] *Ibid.,* p. 142. [3] *Ibid.,* p. 144.

Among the most notable ladies of pleasure flourishing in the twelfth century were Yuya of Ikeda, one-time mistress of Taira Munemori; Senjü of Tagoshi, mistress of Taira Shigehira; and Iso no Zenshi, mistress of Fujiwara Shinsei Shōnagon.[1] Many of these celebrated courtesans, who may be said to have occupied a position in Japanese society equal to that held by the *hetæræ* of ancient Greece, were known by names of a glamorous and ornate character, thus: "The Flower Pass," "Blossom," "Evening Mist," "Street of Flowers," "Cherry Tree," "The Face of Evening," "A Thousand Springs," "White Jewel," "A Moor on a Spring Night,"[1] others of a like nature; while the brothels to which they were attached had equally captivating names, "House of the Eight Banners," "House of the Myriad Flowers," "House of the Long Blooming Flowers," and "House of Ten Thousand Plums"[1] being typical.

Among the less expensive prostitutes were some of the females attached to the bath-houses, which were really houses of assignation, the term bath-house being little more than a euphemism. These attendants, known as "shampooers," were girls or young women of exceptional beauty and charm, and constituted serious rivals to the most accomplished and lovely inmates of the brothels proper.

The lowest class of prostitutes to be found in the Yoshiwara, says the novelist Kyóden (quoted by the author of *The Nightless City*), were accustomed to "lie in wait for passers-by, and pulling in any likely patron they could find would slam to the door. A few minutes afterwards the door would reopen and the guest depart, and this process would be repeated *ad infinitum*."[2]

In the early decades of the twentieth century the popularity of the Yoshiwara showed signs of declining. To some extent

[1] *Notes on the History of the Yoshiwara of Yedo,* 1894.
[2] *The Nightless City,* p. 73.

this was no doubt due to the increased restrictions to which the girls were subjected. The taboo on the display of their charms at the open windows of the houses had some effect. But the main cause, which applies increasingly in Japan as elsewhere, was the competition of the amateur. Today the regulations respecting prostitution generally have been tightened: brothels are now prohibited, professional women are registered, and there are special rules respecting the compulsory treatment of those suffering from venereal disease. The Yoshiwara in Tokyo was closed a few years ago.

Turning to other parts of the Far East, it is to be remarked that the prostitute quarter in Singapore is notorious. In Malay Street even in recent years there have been at one time some five hundred brothels, each holding from eight to thirty girls. These girls displayed themselves on the balconies attached to the houses. "From three o'clock in the afternoon until ten or eleven o'clock in the evening," write the authors of *The White Slave Market,* "the poor, painted creatures, bedecked in their tinsel, sit sipping coffee, smoking cigarettes, and accosting passers-by with the invitation 'come in here, please.' These prostitutes are one of the sights of the East, and strange though it may seem no tourist who visits Singapore dreams of leaving without at least driving through Malay Street to gaze at these 'show women' of every nationality."[1]

In ancient China the prostitute's life was not looked upon as one of shame. The leading members of the profession were equivalent to the *hetæræ* of ancient Greece. This attitude towards the prostitute did not persist through the ages however as in the neighbouring empire of Japan: the day came when the lady of easy virtue was looked upon with loathing and

[1] Mrs Archibald Mackirdy and W. N. Willis, *The White Slave Market*, Stanley Paul, London, n.d., p. 123.

contempt. Moreover, it was seldom that any brothel inmate re-entered respectable society.

In addition to the ordinary houses of prostitution there was a type of brothel peculiar to China: the famous flower boat, with its flower girls. In particular the flower boats of Canton gained a great reputation among men accustomed to consort with prostitutes.

In the old days it was the universal custom for parents who wished to be rid of their female children to sell them to the brothel-owners when they were young, sometimes at birth. Such girls were trained in the prostitute's art. As in Japan, when the supply of girls that were purchasable or who could be enticed into the brothels by fair means was exhausted, it was customary to resort to kidnapping. This practice persisted through the ages. Williams refers to it in the following words: "... brothels and their inmates occur everywhere on land and water. One danger attending young girls going abroad alone is that they will be stolen for incarceration in these gates of hell."[1]

It was stated, in relation to the situation in the city of Hong Kong, that in the middle of last century the girls in the brothels were all young. "They come to Hong Kong at thirteen or fourteen, and are deflowered for a special price, which goes to the owners. No woman is kept in the first-class Chinese house after twenty-four years of age. Then if they are not married, the parents take them away. What becomes of them is not known. They become perhaps hairdressers, servants, or prostitutes in other brothels."[2]

Rarely were these brothel prostitutes given any wages, and in cases where an honorarium was handed out the charges for food and clothing more than absorbed any earnings, so that

[1] S. Wells Williams, *The Middle Kingdom*, Wiley & Putman, New York, 1858, Vol. II., p. 96.

[2] *Correspondence Respecting the Alleged Existence of Chinese Slavery in Hong Kong.*

girls were perpetually in debt to the owner. It is the old, old story as exemplified in every country where brothels are to be found. In a report dated November 2, 1866, it was stated:

"There is another matter connected with the brothels, licensed and unlicensed, in Hong Kong which almost daily assumes a graver aspect. I refer to what is no less than the trafficking in human flesh between the brothel-keepers and the vagabonds of the Colony. Women are bought and sold in nearly every brothel in the place. They are induced by specious pretexts to come to Hong Kong, and then, after they are admitted into the brothels, such a system of espionage is kept over them, and so frightened do they get, as to prevent any application to the police. They have no relatives, no friends to assist them, and their life is such that, unless goaded into unusual excitement by a long course of ill-treatment, they sink down under the style of life they are forced to adopt, and submit patiently to their masters. But cases have occurred where they have run away, and placed themselves in the hands of the police; who, however, can do nothing towards punishing the offenders for the lack of evidence, the women being afraid to tell their tale in open court. Women have, it is true, willingly allowed themselves to be sold for some temporary gain; but that brothel-keepers should be allowed to enter into such transactions is of serious moment."[1]

The evidence presented in the courts in connection with the prosecution of brothel-owners gives a picture of the manner in which recruits were obtained and the conditions under which they lived. Thus William King, inspector of brothels, declared: "I found six girls in the house and three children. The floor was very crowded, and seemed fitted up like a

[1] *Correspondence Respecting the Alleged Existence of Chinese Slavery in Hong Kong.*

barracoon. There were no gratings to the windows. Four of the girls were in a room to themselves at the back of the house. They were all huddled up together and seemed frightened." Lo-ming said. "I am a jeweller and watch repairer residing at No. 70 Wellington-street. I have resided here about three or four years. I know the first defendant. She lives opposite to me at 71 Wellington-street. She has lived there some years, on the first floor. I have consequently seen a number of girls going into and out of the house. They seemed to arrive by steamer, some in chairs and some walking. I know that the defendant, from what I have seen of her and the girls whom I have seen going out of the house, was a buyer and seller of young girls to go to Macao." Then there was the evidence of Wong-Yau: "I am nineteen years of age. I am a native of Wong-chun in Tong-koon district. In consequence of a quarrel between myself and another wife of my husband, he sold me to the defendant, Sz-Sham, for $81. That was only a few days ago. Sz-Sham brought me to Hong Kong by steamer. She took me to A-Neung's house. I have been there ever since. Several men have been up to the house to see me. They were going to buy me if they liked me. I don't know if they looked at any of the other girls."[1]

Women and girls of nationalities other than Chinese were to be found in the brothels of Hong Kong. According to the authors of *The White Slave Market,* "Hundreds of American girls pass through Gage Street and Lyndhurst Terrace during the year, and, if they live, eventually find themselves, when their bloom is gone, and they become addicted to drink and drugs, in the Chinese quarter in Takkn Road, where nearly three hundred brothels exist, each house containing from a dozen to twenty unfortunates of all colours, creeds and castes."

[1] *Correspondence Respecting the Alleged Existence of Chinese Slavery in Hong Kong.*

No system of medical inspection was ever practised in China, either in relation to the brothel inmates or the street girls. As a result there was much disease.

More than one authority has affirmed that opium smoking has a good deal to do with the widespread practice of prostitution by the Chinese, and even more so with the prevalence of sexual perversion. Libermann, for one, asserts that homosexuality was not practised to any considerable extent until opium smoking became popular. This assertion is by no means so far-fetched as might at first sight appear. Opium has acquired a reputation as an aphrodisiac, a reputation which, it may be said, is to a certain extent justified. For the drug does undoubtedly stimulate sexual appetite. At the same time however the continued use of opium or its derivatives unquestionably affects potency, with the result that sooner or later the addict is in the terrible position of having an abnormally developed appetite which he is unable to satisfy by any normal means. Inevitably he turns to perverse practices.

This was one of the reasons for male prostitution becoming so prevalent in China. Boy prostitutes were notorious.

In later years the Chinese authorities did all in their power to restrict the incidence of prostitution in all its forms, and they undoubtedly almost entirely succeeded in bringing about the abandonment of some of its worst features, i.e. the kidnapping of young girls by procurers and the lifelong slavery of brothel prostitution. As long ago as 1910 a decree prohibiting the sale and kidnapping of children for the purpose of prostitution was issued by the Ching Dynasty. Steps towards the abolition of child slavery were taken by the National Government.

It is, of course, impossible to obtain reliable official information concerning the incidence of prostitution in Red China at the present time. But Shanghai is no longer a byword for vice, and Communist authorities are notoriously anti-erotic.

Among the reforms instituted just before the Chinese Revolution was one intended to prevent any girl being forced into the profession against her will. A licence had to be applied for and it was only issued on the girl herself expressing a desire to be a prostitute. The protection given by this regulation was, however, more apparent than real, as it was customary for the brothel-owner to apply for such a licence, merely submitting a photograph of the girl and a signed document in which she stated her wish to be given a licence and that the application was made by the brothel-owner at her request. It may be assumed that in many instances the girl was by no means a free agent, but was acting under coercion exercised by her parents or possibly by the brothel-owner.

To sample Chinese prostitution today in all its old-time courtesy and style one must repair to Formosa, where it remains widespread and open.

XIII: ATTEMPTS AT SUPPRESSION AND REGULATION

SINCE the first appearance of professional prostitution fugitive efforts have been made to stamp it out of existence. There have always been moralists and others who, for one reason or another, have disagreed with the apologetic argument that prostitution is a necessary evil, and in the main, these members of the opposing party have been responsible for the attempts at suppression.

Punishment by whipping and by various forms of torture was often the means chosen; occasionally prostitutes were driven from the towns and cities and sometimes out of the country; more rarely mayhem and the death penalty were imposed.

The most ancient efforts at suppression of which we have any record appear to be the closing of the Roman brothels by Valentine and the younger Theodocius. Justinian adopted similar measures, and threw all concerned with prostitution into exile, while treating the harlots themselves with considerable leniency and devising means to assist their reformation, as, for instance, in removing all barriers to their marriage and entry into respectability. The Empress Theodora, who was a prostitute herself when Justinian married her, encouraged these reformative measures and built a retreat of some magnificence for the housing of penitent harlots.

The efforts at suppression merely served to drive the trade into the adoption of hole-and-corner methods, and we find in every period of oppression and persecution that prostitution still existed in surreptitious forms, breaking out into the open the moment a more tolerant attitude prevailed.

The toleration of the early Christians caused great extension in both brothel and clandestine prostitution. Then, in the sixth century, Recared, a king of the Visigoths, ordered every prostitute to be punished with three hundred strokes of the whip before being driven out of the city. After this, apart from a few half-hearted attempts at suppression, prostitution flourished gaily in profligate Europe for a matter of five hundred years at the most modest of estimates. There were brothels everywhere, flourishing as baths and under other euphemistic names. Many of the nunneries and monasteries were either brothels or places where perverse sexual acts were openly practised.

Indeed for centuries nearly every European city was overrun with prostitutes. It must be remembered that licentiousness was the rule rather than the exception. Paris swarmed with harlots of every class. So did Rome. So did London. So did Venice. In Strasbourg there were whores openly soliciting in every place of worship.

So we arrive at the reign of Louis IX of France, the first French king to make any really sincere effort to put an end to a state of affairs which was making Paris notorious throughout all the marches of Europe. In 1254 Louis made an edict which imposed exile from France upon every prostitute, every brothel-keeper and every procurer. But the cure, as is so often the case, was found to be a good deal worse than the disease. Women of respectability were, by one means or another, induced to satisfy the appetites of those who had been in the habit of frequenting the brothels. Saint Augustine's old dictum proved true—the virtue of respectable womanhood was safe only so long as professional prostitution existed to satisfy the sexual cravings of mankind. After an experiment extending over a couple of years, Louis removed his edict, and the prostitutes flocked back to the reopened brothels. They were, however, compelled to observe certain rules. They were restricted to specific parts of Paris; they were not allowed to wear meretricious apparel; they were supervised by an official. In short, Louis made an attempt at regulation something after the Roman style, but it proved of small value, and finally it was abolished. Philip, successor to Louis, made fitful attempts to suppress prostitution, but actually they proved of little or no avail.

All these and similar efforts continued to be put into force spasmodically and from time to time. But, as I have already indicated, there was no really serious effort made until the rapid expansion of the incidence of syphilis and the blame for its spreading falling upon the harlots caused general alarm throughout Europe.

The sailors who took part in the expedition of Columbus to the New World are supposed to be responsible for introducing syphilis into Europe on their return to Spain in 1494. While the contention that before this time syphilis was unknown in Europe is extremely dubious, it is certain that in the early fifteen hundreds syphilis and gonorrhoea (the two venereal infections were thought, at that time, to be manifestations of one disease) reached a peak of universality hitherto unknown, spreading rapidly throughout every part of the Continent. While the sailors of Columbus were accused of bringing the infection to Spain, the occupants of the brothels were blamed for spreading it wholesale among the male members of the community. Soon after the commencement of the sixteenth century we find brothels and their inmates being attacked in all the countries of Europe.

Thus in France, in 1560, Charles IX was responsible for an

edict which abolished Parisian brothels, compelling all prostitutes and those connected with the profession to leave the city. In Italy, in 1577, every prostitute and every brothel-keeper were given eight days in which to remove themselves from Catalina, the penalty being whipping for the prostitute and the galleys for the brothel-keepers. In Spain, although prostitutes were allowed in the cities, they were compelled to submit to examination by a physician, and if found to be infected were not allowed to practise their profession.

Naturally, these attempts failed to abolish or even to curtail seriously the incidence or extent of prostitution. They merely sufficed to make both the prostitutes and their clients much more careful, and where brothels were actually abolished secret prostitution took the place of open prostitution. Then, too, the waves of persecution, when and as they arose, brought in their train many evils. The laws against prostitution were made to serve other purposes, and men got rid of their mistresses and concubines by accusing them of being professional harlots and having them banished from the district.

It would serve no useful purpose, and it would prove dreary reading, to trace in detail the many attempts at suppression which were attempted through the centuries. Each period of rigorous persecution was followed, in most cases, by a more tolerant attitude, and thus the history of prostitution in Europe is marked by apparent bursts of the most flagrant licentiousness interposed between apparently more moral times. Whipping and other more cruel forms of punishment, exile, imprisonment were all tried again and again, and just as often they all failed. By the time of the Napoleonic wars it was generally recognised throughout Continental Europe that all attempts to suppress the trade were futile.

In America, however, and in England, the moral and religious elements had not given up the fight for suppression. As late as 1891 an attempt was made to clear out the prostitutes in Pittsburgh and in New York City. The brothels and assignment houses were closed, the prostitutes were turned into the streets and tradespeople and landladies were requested to refuse to provide them with either food or lodgings. These measures were drastic and they were cruel, but they failed to produce any permanent good effects—all they did was to drive the women to other towns for the time being.

In England, during the nineteenth century, an attempt at suppression was made at Portsmouth. An account of this effort was given by a witness before the Select Committee appointed in 1879 to inquire into the operation and effects of the Contagious Diseases Acts, and from this account, as given by Havelock Ellis,[1] it appears that the mayor of that city, in 1860, was evidently imbued with the idea of stamping out the prostitution which, at that time, was rampant. To this end, between three hundred and four hundred prostitutes were driven out of their lodgings into the streets. The workhouse, to which they went for succour, refused to admit them, and so, homeless and hungry, they marched the streets for days on end. No one wanted them. There was no place for them to go. In the end the authorities allowed them to return to their lodgings and to pursue their career. The experiment in suppression was a complete failure.

These American and English experiments seem to have been the last efforts at actual suppression. Their failure marked a universal agreement among the bitterest opponents of prostitution on a policy of despair.

As it became obvious that not only was it quite impossible to suppress prostitution, but that in nearly every instance any attempt at suppression brought in its train evils which were at least as bad as the disease itself, the thoughts of reformers and moralists gradually turned from suppression to regula-

[1] Havelock Ellis, *Studies in the Psychology of Sex*, Vol. VI, Davis, Philadelphia, 1927, p. 248.

tion. It was contended that an evil which could not be eradicated was best controlled. Of course efforts at suppression and regulation were for a long time contemporaneous.

We have seen that the regulation of prostitution and the licensing of brothels extend as far back as the time of Solon, and that in various cities of Europe certain regulations were imposed upon brothels and their inmates. But all such attempts at regulation, arising out of religious prostitution, were mainly concerned with raising money for the Church or the State. Eighteenth-century regulation was concerned primarily with health and the morals of the community, and only secondarily and incidentally with taxation.

It is true that after the spread of syphilis in Europe some feeble, fitful, half-hearted attempts had been made in the way of medically examining prostitutes but these measures were not adopted to any serious extent or with any degree of thoroughness. It was not until the eighteenth century that anything in this line worthy of consideration was attempted. Various authorities and various countries have been credited with inaugurating the system of medical examination which was eventually to spread throughout most of Continental Europe, but the truth of the matter seems to be that most countries awoke to the need for some such system about the same time. Thus in Berlin an enactment of 1700, dealing with prostitution, made provision for all professional harlots to be examined by a surgeon once a fortnight. In 1724 Bernard Mandeville, an English writer, in his notorious pamphlet *A Modest Defence of Publick Stews,* advocated the medical inspection of prostitutes frequenting brothels, but his arguments were received without approval. All this time prostitution was increasing; and all this time, too, venereal disease was spreading by leaps and bounds. By the end of the century, through the incidence of the French Revolution and the series of wars it brought in its train, syphilis and gonorrhoea were rampant, and prostitutes flaunted their charms brazenly in every big city of Europe.

The first attempt at registration in France was the system introduced in 1778, but it was Napoleon, at the height of his fame and power, who was responsible for the establishment in Paris of the first really adequate system of medical examination of prostitutes. Actually, the system was first introduced in 1802, but it was not until some twenty years later that it was perfected and became in general use throughout the Parisian brothels. This French system, it is worthy of mention, was not based upon a law applying universally to all towns, cities, *et al.* Each municipal authority was empowered to take such steps as were deemed advisable in the interests of public order and health. It is for this reason that regulation was not in force in every French city at that time.

A description of the procedure in regard to registration is given by Acton. He says: "The registration is now either on the voluntary demand of the female or by requisition of the *Bureau des Mœurs.* On appearing before this tribunal, the candidate, after declaring her name, age, quality, birthplace, occupation and domicile, is submitted to a searching examination, as follows. Is she married or single? Has she father and mother living, and what are their pursuits? Does she reside with them; if not, why not, and when did she leave them? Has she children? How long has she inhabited Paris, and can she be owned there? Has she ever been arrested, and if so, the particulars? Has she previously been a prostitute? If so, the details? Has she had any, and what, education? Has she had any venereal affection? Her motives for the step? She next proceeds to the *Bureau Sanitaire,* is medically examined, and enrolled in that department. If found diseased, she is consigned to the Saint-Lazare Hospital forthwith. Steps are meanwhile taken to verify her replies at the *Bureau des Mœurs,* and formal communications are now made to the mayor of her native commune, with an appeal for the woman's redemption to her parents."[1]

When a prostitute was licensed to carry out her profession, she was given a card, bearing on one side her name, address and registered number, and on the other blank spaces for entering the dates of medical inspection. These registrations were termed voluntary, but in reality, in the majority of cases, it was a matter of *force majeure*. The unregistered prostitute had a hard time of it; she was continually exercising vigilance to escape the attentions of the police.

In 1946 new laws dealing with prostitution came into force in France, by which *maisons de tolérance* were prohibited. A form of regulation continued, however, in so much that all prostitutes were inscribed and must submit themselves for medical examination at regular intervals. Even so, there is inevitably a considerable amount of clandestine prostitution, and with the ever-increasing number of amateur prostitutes it becomes more and more difficult, in any country where a system of registration is in force, to distinguish between the professional who is pursuing her calling clandestinely and the amateur. At the same time, owing to the animosity towards all rivals displayed somewhat naturally by the inscribed woman, the position is not without its dangers to the freedom of the individual, and a girl who might originally have no intention of emerging from "amateur prostitution" or even "occasional prostitution" may be induced by the police to submit to registration.

In England many attempts have been made to institute a system of regulation. The earliest of these attempts of which there is any record was the sanctioning by Parliament in 1161 of the establishment of brothels ("stews") in the city of London, where they were permitted to flourish for nearly four

[1] William Acton, *Prostitution Considered in its Moral, Social and Sanitary Aspects*, pp. 103-4.

hundred years. Public opinion in Great Britain has always been against the regulation or the licensing of prostitutes, largely because it is felt that any such regulation amounts to a justification of the evil. This attitude on the part of the English people and the English government has been considered, by foreigners, to be a hypocritical attitude. And, admittedly, so it is. But hypocritical or not, the English people may be considered to be definitely opposed to any system of licensing and medical inspection. For the licensing system *has* been tried in England. The experiment, now long forgotten, is of such importance in any study of prostitution that it is worthy of consideration in some detail.

The reason for the putting into operation of this system of licensing was through the fact that a committee was appointed by the Admiralty in 1862 to consider the question of venereal disease in the Army and Navy, and the regulation of prostitution. This committee's findings were against the compulsory medical examination of prostitutes, but they considered that it would be advisable to take steps to induce these women to submit voluntarily to examination and, if diseased, to enter special hospitals for treatment. However, these details were not presented to the public; but when, on June 20, 1864, Lord Clarence Paget, Secretary to the Admiralty, presented the Bill which was later to be the subject of such widespread public indignation and bitter controversy, in the debate in the House of Commons the grave state of health in the Army and Navy generally through the ravages of venereal infections was the justification given for the measures embodied in the proposed Act. The Bill, known as the Contagious Diseases Prevention Act, 1864, was finally placed upon the statute book in July of that year.

Briefly stated, the Act provided for the compulsory examination of any woman believed to be "a common prostitute," and if found to be suffering from a venereal disease, for her detention in a Lock hospital for a period not exceeding three months. The Act applied to the garrison towns of Portsmouth, Plymouth, Woolwich, Chatham, Sheerness, Aldershot, Colchester, Shorncliffe, the Curragh, Cork and Queenstown —the idea of its promoters was to give it a three years' trial. Two years later a further Act was passed to take effect on the expiration of the 1864 Act. This new Act extended the features of the existent one, by providing for the registration of prostitutes and their compulsory regular medical examination, thus embodying the main features of the registration system in vogue in so many Continental States. It also added Windsor to the list of towns. Then in 1869, another Act added Canterbury, Dover, Gravesend, Maidstone, Winchester and Southampton to the list.

The Acts were not operated by the ordinary police. A special body of plain-clothes officers were embodied in each of the towns in which the Acts applied. Virtually these officials were private detectives, and their duties consisted in discovering any women who were engaged in professional promiscuity. Every woman who was found to be a prostitute had her name and address entered upon a special register, and once a name was entered it could not be removed without permission. The object of this register was to place in the hands of the police a means whereby known prostitutes could be compelled to present themselves at regular intervals for medical examination. Thus once a fortnight each woman whose name appeared on the register must submit to medical inspection or become liable to arrest and imprisonment. So long as the registered woman remained healthy she was allowed to ply her trade; if on examination, she proved to be infected with syphilis, gonorrhœa or soft chancre (the three contagious venereal infections), she was packed off to a hospital where she was to all intents and purposes a prisoner. And there she was detained until supposedly cured of the infection.

The special body of police in plain clothes who administered the law made every effort to "find" women who made a profession of prostitution, and, when found, to force them to sign what was termed a "voluntary submission". The signing of this form by any woman amounted to an admission that she was a prostitute, and an undertaking to present herself for fortnightly medical examination. Once signed there was no such thing as retraction—even the giving up of prostitution in favour of regular respectable employment or of marriage was not in itself sufficient to render her free from the necessity of presenting herself for examination.

There can be no question whatever but that the Acts led to wholesale injustice, as anyone with experience of the workings of officialdom in any part of the world can very well imagine. The police bullied the girls and women into signing the form, and, as they never explained the nature of its contents, and as, further, in those days, the bulk of women of the servant and peasant class were unable to read, in very many instances they had not the slightest conception of what they were signing.

Naturally enough the Acts and the manner of carrying out their provisions came in for a considerable amount of criticism, and gradually there sprang up in the country a good deal of hostile feeling. As a result of this controversy and the continually growing distaste for the official bullying and interference, two associations were formed with the specific common object of securing the repeal of the Acts. Many prominent men and women worked tooth and nail to this end, foremost among whom were Daniel Cooper, James Stansfield, Florence Nightingale, Harriett Martineau and Josephine Butler. Even so, progress was slow and wearisomely difficult, and it was not until 1886 that the Acts were actually repealed.

Although there have always been, and there are today, plenty of English legislators and reformers in favour of the regulation of prostitution, since that day no serious attempt has been made to reintroduce any system of registration and medical examination of prostitutes. For the ill-starred wartime measure of 1918 and the somewhat similar regulation of 1942 can hardly be dignified by inclusion in the category of systems for the regulation of prostitution.[1]

Turning to the United States of America, it appears that an initial attempt at regulation was made about the same time as the English experiment. A colonel of the United States Army, one Fletcher, attached to the Surgeon-General's Office, and who claimed to be the first to attempt any "systematic inspection of prostitutes" in the United States, along with another medical officer, at Nashville, in 1863, instituted a system, which operated for three years, whereby public women were compelled to present themselves for medical examination at ten-day intervals.

The next attempt at regulation, on the lines advocated by Sanger himself, who was strongly in favour of the licensing

[1] Owing to venereal disease in the army reaching such enormous proportions, in 1918 a regulation (40d), dealing with diseased prostitutes, was added to the Defence of the Realm Act. It empowered the authorities to force any woman to submit herself to medical examination if accused by a member of H.M.Forces of having infected him with a venereal disease. It presented, obviously, opportunities for vindictive allegations and gross injustice. It was repealed within a year of adoption.

In 1942 during the Second World War, the Ministry of Health introduced a regulation (33b) which provided that in the event of two or more patients who were being treated for venereal disease naming the *same* individual as the source of their infection, that particular individual should be ordered to undergo examination and submit to treatment until free from infection. Failure to do so was punishable with imprisonment, or fine, or both. The Act was obviously aimed mainly at professional prostitutes. True, it could be applied to other women and also to men, but any such case was unlikely. Such a regulation opened up possibilities of blackmail and malicious secret information, and could not possibly prove anything more than a palliative, and a very poor and largely ineffective one at that. It expired at the end of 1947.

of prostitutes and their systematic medical inspection, was made in 1872, in the middle-western city of St Louis. All women engaged in the profession of prostitution, whether they were brothel inmates, street-walkers or mistresses, were compelled to be registered and to submit to weekly inspection. If once a woman was entered on the register she must notify the police on making any change of address, whether within the city of St Louis or elsewhere. The statute was, however, short-lived, lasting barely a year. So strong was the opposition to what was described by its opponents as "the licensing of vice" that, after the presentation of a petition bearing over a hundred thousand signatures, the authorities were compelled to remove the statute.

Since that day no general attempt has been made to reintroduce the registration of prostitutes, but the famous Page law of 1910 contains a clause (Section 79) providing for the medical examination of any prostitute convicted as a vagrant.

As we have seen, today there are few American or Canadian cities with "red-light" districts, these having been abolished in deference to public opinion. Before the First World War, practically every city of any size in the United States had its "red-light" district. The abolition of brothels and houses of assignation blatantly proclaiming their trade does not, however, imply their non-existence, any more than it does in English cities. They flourish in innumerable surreptitious forms, and they secure their clientele through "underground" channels or by means of carefully worded advertisements. In particular, of course, there has been developed to a high degree the "call-girl" system, in which the customer telephones a bureau organised for the purveying of vice, with details of his requirements.

No survey of the world position would be complete without a glance at what happened in the U.S.S.R. when, in 1922, the campaign against prostitution was inaugurated. The most remarkable, unique and albeit highly commendable feature of this struggle was that the women engaged in the profession were not proceeded against in any punitive or retributive way. On the contrary, the proceedings were instituted against those who exploited the prostitutes (the pimps, procurers, brothel-keepers and other traffickers in vice), and these proceedings were carried out rigorously. In addition, the names and addresses of men found consorting with prostitutes were publicly displayed. Acting on the assumption that unemployment was the main factor in the creation of the prostitute, measures were taken to obtain work for all females capable of engaging in it, and to provide special facilities for the education and training (with pay) of prostitutes so they could take up technical or professional work. Simultaneously early marriages were encouraged, absolute equality of the sexes admitted, and the ignominy, stigma or ostracism formerly connected with illegitimacy was swept away.[1]

---

[1] In Freed's interesting and valuable study of prostitution in Johannesburg we read: "It appears to be possible that illegitimacy is very frequently the first stage on the road to prostitution" (Louis Franklin Freed, *The Problem of European Prostitution in Johannesburg*, 1949, p. 164).

PART THREE

PROSTITUTION TODAY

XIV: MODERN PRACTITIONERS OF THE OLDEST PROFESSION

PROFESSIONAL prostitution today exists in many forms, the precise form or forms flourishing in different countries, and in different parts of the same country, varying considerably. For instance, there are no brothel prostitutes in England, as there are in various foreign countries. On the other hand, street-walkers, who used to be so common in some English cities, are rarely seen in many foreign countries. (Nowadays, of course, prostitutes are not allowed to solicit openly in the streets in England). Then again, in some States, prostitutes are registered, in others there is no system of regulation whatsoever. Usually, brothels and registration go together, though there are registered prostitutes who are not inmates of brothels or in any way connected with them. It would appear to be customary in all regulationist countries (i.e. countries where there is a system of registration and medical inspection) to regard prostitution as an evil which must be endured; and in all abolitionist countries (i.e. countries where there is no registration or medical inspection) to ignore the question of prostitution except where and so far as it can be linked with some other offence and penalised or punished vicariously. The modern tendency is undoubtedly against regulation, as is instanced by the steady decline in the number of countries adopting registration.

In a few countries the authorities have gone much further than the actual prohibition of brothels, and have made prostitution *in itself* a breach of the law, while in others, including some countries where brothels are permitted, the act of solicitation is punishable.

In Europe only two regulationist countries remain: Turkey (where there are about three hundred *maisons tolérées*) and Austria.[1] In the latter, curiously enough, the houses exist in the large provincial cities only, and not in Vienna itself. In Innsbruck, for instance, there are two establishments side by side only a hundred yards or so from the station, each with a workaday porter outside, dressed in ordinary clothes, but with a peaked cap bearing the gilt letters *Portier*. On the entry of a client an aged crone will clap her hands and a dozen girls and women of uncertain charms will come helter-skelter down the stairs for inspection. These houses seem scrupulously clean, and carry long official printed notices on the walls of the bedrooms.

The countries where brothels are tolerated are gradually becoming fewer. In 1950 they were: Algeria, Arabia, Argentina,[2] Bolivia, Chile, China, Colombia, Costa Rica, Ecuador, Egypt, Eritrea, Ethiopia, French Cameroons, Greece, Guatemala, Haiti, certain Provinces in India, Indo-china, Iraq, Italy, Korea, Lebanon, Martinique, Morocco, parts of Mexico, Nicaragua, Peru, Portugal, Senegal, Somaliland, Spain, Syria, Thailand, Tunisia, Turkey and Uruguay.[3] Since then some of these have abolished brothels, including Spain (consequent upon pressure from those connected with American service-

---

[1] *L'Esclavage de la Femme*, by Odette Philippon, Paris, 1960.

[2] For interesting details about prostitution in Central and South America see *The Americas after Dark*, edited by Eugene Cramond, illustrated, Tallis Press, 9/6d.

[3] From the pamphlet entitled *Situation Abolitioniste Mondiale*, published by the International Abolitionist Federation, Geneva, Switzerland, 1951.

men stationed there!) and Portugal, plus, of course, China. The famous French brothels were closed soon after the Second World War. In 1957 the Wolfenden Report indicated that there were then only nineteen countries with tolerated brothels as against one hundred and nineteen abolitionist countries.

Most of, if not all, the systems of registration and examination are founded upon that which was in vogue in France for so many generations. There are variations, of course. For instance, in some countries all the prostitutes are inmates of brothels; in others while there are no brothels, the women are all compelled to submit to registration and examination.

Of all classes of prostitutes those who live in brothels are the most slave-like, and, apart from a few old raddled and diseased harlots who infest the poorest parts of the cities, they earn the smallest sums of money. True, the brothel is often a most profitable affair, but little of this profit is garnered by the harlots attached to it. The usual practice is for each girl to receive a percentage of the fees she earns, which are fixed fees and paid to the head of the establishment, usually an aged procurer referred to as the *Madame*. Against these earnings the girl has to pay for her clothes, perfumes, etc.—costly items, the money for which in the first instance is advanced to her by the management. Often, too, she has to pay for her food. As a rule, in the end, there is little for her to draw and often she is perpetually in debt to the house. The life is a hard one, as the girl is not allowed any choice as regards the type of men or the number of men she associates with—she is compelled to serve all comers and at all times.

In the houses of assignation, which were so numerous in Paris and many other Continental cities, the prostitute was much freer, and usually earned much more money. She was, like the brothel prostitute, in the employment of the management and working on a percentage basis, but she had to be available at certain times only, after which she was free to go to her home.

Many of the brothels and houses of assignation which still exist largely rely upon touts to secure clients. These touts are usually chauffeurs, waiters, bartenders, barbers, garage workers and others, who are likely to come into contact with large numbers of men and particularly with commercial travellers and visitors to the city. They work on commission. In many cases a stranger finds it difficult to make the acquaintance of a prostitute except through one of these intermediaries. In most cities which still provide specific "red-light" districts, whether the brothels are openly conducted or are "underground" affairs, the employment of touts or other intermediaries is a common practice. In certain dubious hotels, such as there are for the finding in most of the larger cities in all countries the world over, there is sometimes an arrangement whereby, on request, girls of easy virtue can be readily secured.

Then there are the registered prostitutes who are not attached to either brothels or houses of assignation. They work on the streets, in the café-bars and the night clubs. All they earn is their own, and, to a certain extent, they are free to pick and choose their men. They are, however, continually harassed in other ways. They must keep within certain specified districts; they must solicit at certain specified times, and at these times only; and they are often subjected to demands from the police which are little removed from blackmail.[1] It is largely from the ranks of these free-lances that the brothel harlots are recruited. A girl falls on bad times, she cannot meet the heavy expenses which her mode of life entails, she is

---

[1] The prevalence of blackmail constitutes one of the major evils in connection with prostitution. The peculiar reaction of society and the law to this particular social phenomenon creates, encourages and develops blackmail. The evil applies in every country, regulationist or non-regulationist.

weary of the continual police interference—in sheer desperation she enters a brothel.

The unregistered women are known as clandestine prostitutes. In a country which has a system of licensing there are not supposed to be any prostitutes other than registered women, but in actual fact there are large numbers who are unregistered.[1] This is true of every country the world over. It is quite impossible, however stringent are the regulations, however vigilant are the police, to prevent unregistered or clandestine prostitutes from plying their trade. The reasons for this are many. The majority of women do not wish to be branded as prostitutes; nor do they wish to submit to the indignity and trouble of regular medical inspection. They may wish at some later date to marry, or to enter some other profession, and the stigma which attaches for life to the registered prostitute is the very thing they are anxious at all costs to avoid.

It is owing to the huge proportion of clandestine harlots that it is impossible to gauge with any pretension to accuracy the number of prostitutes in any country, any city or any town. The figures issued by various official and social organisations, and which are quoted in books and pamphlets, are mainly guesswork. They are as much guesswork as applied to cities where registration is in force as they are in relation to those where there is no such thing as registration.

A noticeable feature in recent years has been the marked number of exceedingly young prostitutes. There is no doubt whatever that today prostitutes commence their careers at earlier ages than they did in previous generations. This is doubtless a result of the remarkable precocity of youth which is such a feature of the age we live in.

---

[1] It may safely be asserted that in all countries where a system of registration is in force the number of clandestine prostitutes is to the number of registered prostitutes in the ratio of ten to one.

The young prostitute almost invariably possesses an added attractiveness in the eyes of the average man. Few of those looking for a girl fail to be tempted by youth or the appearance of youth, and, especially, by virginity. We have seen that in ancient times and among savages the possession of virginity was not considered to be of any great value and in some cases was to be despised; but in these civilised days an intact hymen is thought a great deal of by the man who is looking for a *prostitute* to act as a sleeping partner, little as he is actually likely to find it. It is, for one thing, almost a one-hundred-percent guarantee against venereal infection. For another thing, to many men intercourse with a virgin approximates to marriage. So prized an asset is virginity *in a prostitute* that in brothels the fee demanded in the case of a virgin is invariably considerably higher than that asked for where an experienced prostitute is concerned. All of which has led to the simulation of virginity, which is by no means so difficult a procedure as would at first sight appear. Often an astringent solution, such as alum, dissolved in water, or vinegar, is used to tighten up the relaxed vaginal walls, and a simulacrum of the virginal haemorrhage is produced by arranging the "deflowering" to occur during the menstrual period. An old trick, mentioned by Erich Wulffen (*Woman as a Sexual Criminal*, Ethnological Press, New York, 1934), which provided the bloody discharge that is expected to accompany defloration, consisted of blistering the vagina by the application of leeches —these blisters, engorged with blood, burst during coitus. The same writer also refers to the surreptitious sprinkling of the sheets with pigeon's blood; an old and favourite method bearing points of resemblance to the ingenious device for providing signs of virginity used in "Mrs Cole's" eighteenth-century brothel and described in John Cleland's erotic work *Memoirs of Fanny Hill*.[1] In some cases surgical measures are

---

[1] Available as a paperback, Luxor Press, 9/6d.

resorted to, the hymenal opening being reduced to the virginal one-finger dimensions by suturing.

It is highly probable that the number of prostitutes fluctuates from time to time in accordance with the prosperity of the country. It is affected, too, by other special circumstances; such, for instance, as the movements of large bodies of men and the outbreak of war. During the European conflict of 1914-18, and again during the Second World War, the number of prostitutes in French and English cities far exceeded those in evidence at any other time; and for several years after the cessation of hostilities the boom in trade was responsible for much prosperity among the prostitutes of New York, London, Paris and many smaller cities throughout the world. Equally, depressions and crisis conditions can have their effects. In Berlin, during the extraordinary inflation of the early 1920's, when money became virtually valueless, plenty of respectable women were forced on to the streets for mere existence, and could be seen openly soliciting, many with whips in their hands. In Germany again, after the end of the war in 1945, and when conditions were appalling, the price of a woman to occupying troops was three cigarettes.

Prostitutes of certain nationalities show a marked preference for following in the wake of their own countrymen; in certain cases they are encouraged to do so by the authorities concerned. Thus, in some circumstances, a government will encourage the emigration of, and, if necessary, will actually provide, women for the use of its nationals in foreign countries.[1] This was particularly the case in the East.

Every big city attracts prostitutes because these women are well aware that wherever men forgather in numbers there are potential clients. The fact that in some cities prostitutes may

[1] Usually this policy is associated with the prohibition of intercourse with native or foreign women, as many men show a preference for women of another nationality.

not appear to be present in such profusion or may not parade themselves so blatantly as in others does not mean they are not to be found: it merely means that the by-laws or regulations are such that soliciting or loitering on the streets would be risky or dangerous. In most cities where soliciting is prevalent there are certain well-known streets or localities which the prostitutes frequent and where their clients look for them. At one time or another (either pre-war or post-war) for instance, the Unter den Linden and Friedrichstrasse in Berlin; the St Pauli district in Hamburg (here, a large showcase building devoted to prostitutes has just been erected); the Place Pigalle and the Place Blanche in the Montmartre of Paris, and Rue St Denis,[1] the Kärntnerstrasse in Vienna; the vicinity of Gare du Nord in Brussels; near Blythswood Square in Glasgow; the Sixth and Seventh Avenues in the neighbourhood of 42nd Street, New York. In Amsterdam remains one of the curious sights of Europe: many little rooms, usually at ground level, along the canals adjacent to the Oude Kerk (old Church), at the windows of which girls sit waiting for customers. There are a couple of small similar streets in The Hague, also in Belgium at Antwerp, where the women are of an incredible age—all seem to be over seventy—, and in Germany at Aachen.

In view of the fact that social habits can quickly get lost from memory unless recorded, it is useful to detail the situation in London in the years just prior to the passing of the Street Offences Act, 1959, which changed the face of London as far as street-walkers were concerned. The following notes, written in 1953, were kindly made available by a client of prostitutes who prefers to remain anonymous: [2]

[1] Up to the advent of General de Gaulle in 1958 this street was lined with girls: on Saturdays and Sundays there was absolutely a regiment of them in the Rue St Denis and the little streets off it—now, they have virtually all vanished.

[2] One who was courageous enough not to conceal his interest in

"In London, Hyde Park, as in earlier times[1] remains a haunt of the ladies of the town. There are three main beats: along the South Carriage-road behind Knightsbridge Barracks; on the most westerly path parallel to the East Carriage-road[2] and sometimes in that road itself near Grosvenor Gate, and along the North Ride, parallel to Bayswater Road. Occasionally one or two can also be found strolling along the Ride, which exits at Victoria Gate.

During the afternoon the only beats in use are those in the South Carriage-road and the North Ride, the usual fee being two pounds, plus the cost of a taxi-ride to the girl's room in South Kensington, Paddington or wherever it may be. The East Carriage-road area is only in use in the evening, when motor-cars stop and a girl sitting on the public seat will walk across and get in the car. After a short discussion the girl will get out and the car move off, or the man and the girl will drive off together, according to her success in arranging terms. When darkness falls some girls are prepared to undertake *coitus in statione* (coitus standing up) for a pound, or two pounds for ordinary coitus if the car is used—a curious surcharge considering that the client is providing the facilities.

The path referred to above is used only at night, when in an atmosphere of flitting forms, comprising prostitutes of both sexes, prospective clients, 'peeping toms,' and, of course, innocent passers-by, *coitus in statione* is arranged,

frail ladies was the late Clarkson Rose, the famous entertainer, who gave in his autobiography interesting details of the celebrated lounge of the old Empire Theatre in Leicester Square, a haunt of the *demimonde*.

[1] Hyde Park was a popular Victorian place for fornicators, as is related in *Walter: My Secret Life*, edited by Drs Kronhausen (Polybooks, two volumes, 9/6d each).

[2] In the following decade the Knightsbridge Barracks were pulled down and the East Carriage-road replaced by the modern motor road going north adjacent to Park Lane.

usually for the sum of ten shillings, and takes place against a tree. For the indigent, some girls provide the facility of a "play-about" for five shillings.

Meanwhile, numbers of girls will be found patrolling Bayswater Road, congregating at Stanhope Gate, Albion Gate, and the corner of Clarendon Place, and further west, between Leinster Terrace and Queensway. Some of these girls have rooms, for others there is only the open air, and prices vary accordingly, two pounds or thirty shillings in the one case, and a pound in the other. One girl, who employed a hotel room near Paddington, told me she was doing it for a short period only, it being the only way she could think of to collect quickly the deposit she needed to buy a working-class café in Brighton.

In the West End of an afternoon and evening, there are a few girls in Shepherd Market[1] and in Cork Street, Mayfair, but of course in the evenings the number of prostitutes out is vastly increased. They abound in the little streets around Old Bond Street, in Piccadilly even so far west as Down Street, and especially in the streets north of Piccadilly Circus such as Glasshouse Street, Sherwood Street, Denman Street and the entire length of Brewer Street. But by the small hours of the morning exceedingly few girls will be left.

There is a group of girls at the Soho end of Brewer Street, in Wardour Street, Old Compton Street, Romilly Street and the south end of Dean Street. On the south side of Shaftesbury Avenue there are women in Gerrard Street, Lisle Street, Rupert Street and the southern end of Wardour Street. Some of these places also have girls working in the afternoon.

The remaining two main groups are isolated: one near Victoria Station, where a few patrollers survive in the

---

[1] About 1958 prostitutes could be seen nearby in Curzon Street, some of them accosting from their parked motor-cars.

Eccleston Square section of Belgrave Road, (in earlier years they congregated in Milton Road) while the other is in the East End, in Commercial Road.

Mr Basil L. Henriques, J.P., was reported in the *East London Advertiser* in June, 1952, as having counted eighteen prostitutes in Commercial Street between Berner Street and Batty Street, and between Berner Street and Cannon Street Road he said there were fifty to eighty prostitutes. He remarked, 'This is something entirely new to this part of London.' It seems difficult to credit the numbers given by Mr Henriques. Both before and after the date of his inspection, I had investigated this area and usually counted between six and a dozen all told, even on a Saturday night. Mostly their facilities are confined to *coitus in statione* for ten shillings.[1]

In the West End charges vary a lot—as much as four pounds being asked and obtained by the women in the vicinity of Cork Street, while two pounds is the usual fee demanded in the Glasshouse Street area, and it is most unusual to obtain a quotation of less than thirty shillings, for going to a room anywhere. This is the general charge in Soho. A few girls will go 'all night' for five pounds.

The lower end of Rupert Street is largely devoted at night time to taxi women, whose usual fee is thirty shillings, though it may be as high as two pounds. The taxi-driver gets ten shillings of this and drives the couple to a quiet spot such as the cul-de-sac of Suffolk Street near Trafalgar Square, and intercourse takes place on the back seat. Usually the girl takes little clothing off, but I know of one who stripped everything! Another, much less accommodating, expected me to have intercourse while the taxi was going along, a most difficult feat.

[1] Stepney was a notorious place for prostitutes for a long time afterwards.

It is customary for a shrewd client who is going to a room to confirm that the girl will strip. Some refuse to do so altogether, others raise their charge from thirty shillings to two pounds for stripping, while there is a varying interpretation of what stripping means anyway. To some it merely means taking off the dress, leaving on brassière and knickers, others retain a roll-on of specially useful design, while a few—very few—do take everything off. It has to be admitted that most of these girls are extremely lazy and will avoid even the slight amount of work involved in stripping if they can.

The bargain having been struck, the prostitute and her client move off to her room (or the taxi, tree or wall as the case may be), usually at a fast pace, as although she may have been waiting an hour or more for a client, once she has hooked him she is anxious to be done with him as soon as possible. (In fact, she would often solicit by asking 'Would you like a "short-time"?') Diffident customers may walk a yard behind the woman because of her conspicuousness, with her flamboyant dress, gaudy umbrella and high-heeled shoes, not to dwell on hair often dyed to an unnatural colour in blonde and auburn shades. She will unlock the street door and pound upstairs (the prostitute with a ground-floor flat is a *rara avis* indeed), nearly always up several flights of stairs and often to the very top of the building. Here is her bedroom, which is usually joined to a kitchen in which sits the maid.

The prostitute will take her fee, plus a tip for the maid (usually half-a-crown) then both the client and the prostitute get on the bed, usually of double size and covered with a bedspread, and the most notable piece of furniture in the room. Often a divan is employed. The light is virtually invariably left on in the evening. Intercourse takes place after the prostitute has endeavoured by her best

149

means to ensure a quick termination to the coitus. Usually, however, she does not permit the man to handle her genital organs. After the condom has been taken off and the penis wiped with toilet paper or a towel (the latter a most dangerous proceeding because of the risk of venereal disease germs being transferred from one client to another) both dress again and the man is ushered out, followed a minute or two later by the woman who returns to her stance, but often does not like, by departing with him, to remind her customer that he is only one of many.

The room which they have just left is very likely in a poor state of repair, though sometimes flats which are well-furnished may be found. The furniture, apart from the bed, and usually a dressing-table, comprises in most instances only a couple of chairs. In perhaps 10 per cent. of cases there are pictures on the walls of nude women, or women in lingerie, in various 'artistic' poses. For her room the prostitute has to pay an enormous rent—often in the region of £20 per week, and very likely key money up to £150 to get it to start with.

The maid is often an ex-prostitute who is now too old to attract clients, and is kept to avoid acts of sadism by men against the prostitute, as in the past there have been several cases of murder.

Another overhead with which the prostitute has to cope is the fines to which she is subjected: usually the girls are pulled in regularly for a £2 fine. It used to be said that they had to tip the policemen on their beat, or give way to them in physical gratification (see W. Eden Hooper, *The History of Newgate and the Old Bailey*) but this is not an accusation which is heard nowadays. Nevertheless one girl told me that she numbered policemen in off-duty hours among her paying clients.

It can be stated with certainty that by far the larger

proportion of men who patronise prostitutes are the same men all the time; in these circumstances, and considering the value of regular clients, it is extraordinary that the girls —particularly the English ones— make so little endeavour to give satisfaction. A new girl may be very successful for a few weeks owing to the fact that the usual men like a new face, but once they have tried her, custom falls off, and she very likely disappears because she is not making the job pay. Although there are a few who remain on a beat for a considerable period, women are dropping out all the time and new ones coming in.

A really successful prostitute can make a lot of money. One told me that her top score was thirty-seven men in a day at thirty shillings a time, and even if she kept up nothing like this average her income might easily exceed that of the Prime Minister—and all tax-free! This particular girl told me she spent her money gambling.

On the other hand, some girls may go a whole evening without getting a client. A Paddington girl said that the night before I met her she had had all evening only a ten-shilling client—a lorry-driver who could only afford a 'play-about.' Some have day-time jobs; the successful ones do not.

Contrary to widely-held opinion, the average prostitute has very little of unusual interest to offer; the normal girl will not undertake sodomy, flagellation or any of the sex perversions, though some, especially the French girls, offer *fellatio*. Most prostitutes will not even consent to any unusual position in coitus.

Speaking from considerable experience, I can say that the average girl is honest, and will make no attempt to rob or blackmail a client; her main defect is utter lack of hygienic precautions, although practically all insist on use of the condom. This does not apply to the French girls in London, most of whom are not insistent on its use, but these women are, however, very much cleaner than the English ones, and will scrupulously disinfect both their own and their clients' genitals. This applies to an even greater degree in Paris where, of course, because of Catholic influence the condom is not so readily available.

The French are by no means the only foreigners on the streets in London: I have seen even a Japanese girl operating in Soho, and Scottish and Irish girls often crop up. Whatever their nationality, however, the lives they lead seem to have an unpleasant effect on the ladies of the town; their beady, too-bright eyes in search of victims, and their general demeanour always remind me of that bird with a peculiar name in the Zoo—the 'sociable vulture!' "

As a result of the enactment of the Street Offences Act, 1959, with its threat of imprisonment, London became a much cleaner city, and the girls who, before then, had infested Soho, Bayswater Road, Shepherd Market and other places known to the clients of prostitutes, vanished almost overnight. There were a few women who maintained their rooms in alleys, with a Christian name or the word "Model" on a card stuck over the door-bell, and one tried to solicit out of a window in Shepherd Market until her enterprise was quenched by a magistrate, but most of the street-girls seem to give up their life quite quickly. The only effort which maintained a long-term success was by advertising on postcards in the showcases of certain newsagents, particularly in the Bayswater and Kensington areas. Apart from the humdrum references to *"Model" and "Teacher: Strict Disciplinarian"*, some had more original approaches, such as "Lost: a ring inscribed I Love Dick"; "Young girl requires driving-post"; "Pretty coloured pussy for sale"; and, perhaps neatest of all, "Gentlemen's private work done." There would be a telephone number or perhaps an address, usually in a slummy basement. The customer would have very little idea of the quality of the goods he had been to so much trouble to obtain, and certainly could not "shop around" as he might have in the old days.

Needless to say, too, the over-zealous police endeavoured to block even these harmless endeavours by finding some vague law under which to prosecute the offending newsagents, and a publisher of a *Ladies' Directory* was imprisoned.

The occasional street-walker ventures out at night, but nowadays London, like Paris, has lost a lot of its excitement as a result of the passing of the prostitute parade.

There are, in every big city, a few prostitutes who work hand in hand with various types of criminals, notably blackmailers and cardsharpers. After the woman has enticed a client to her room, an "indignant and threatening husband" bursts upon the scene. Eventually, for a monetary consideration, he agrees to overlook the incident. Or the prostitute may introduce her client to some private and exclusive club or other establishment where gaming for high stakes is in progress. Other women make a practice of robbing their clients while they are sleeping, or whenever an opportunity offers. Especially does this apply where the man is drunk. The prostitute has little fear of any charge being brought against her. True, such charges are made occasionally, as the police court reports show,[1] but for every case of robbery where an accusation is lodged against the prostitute who has engineered the robbery there are a hundred cases where the consequent exposure deters the man from mentioning his loss to anybody, least of all the police. In general, however, in most cities, prostitutes are surprisingly content with their fee without resort to blackmailing or robbery.

---

[1] There have even been instances where girls have been convicted of false pretences through taking money in London clubs without giving the sexual intercourse they promised!

XV: THE COMPETITION OF THE
AMATEUR PROSTITUTE

In addition to the women who are entirely dependent for their bread and butter on their earnings from the hire of their bodies, there are large and ever-increasing numbers who have other means of earning part or all of their livelihood, and who indulge in promiscuous sexual intercourse as a means of supplementing their incomes. These are prostitutes in all but name.

These amateurs for generations have flourished prominently in all big towns and cities. Sixty or seventy years ago the shopgirls very often supplemented wages which were insufficient to feed and clothe them adequately with money earned on the streets. Many cheap chorus girls and unknown actresses, from the days when theatres and music-halls were born, secured the bulk of their meretricious finery by just this means.

Today, true enough, in all walks of life, earnings are very much better than in earlier times. Few girls, from sheer necessity, need to walk the streets. But, paradoxical as it may seem, there are far more amateur prostitutes today than there ever were before. They exist in every stratum of society, and the fact that these girls would burst into hot anger at the mere suggestion that they were prostituting their bodies does not alter the fact that they are, in everything except name, morally indistinguishable from the most brazen harlots.

The reasons for this vast development of amateur prostitution are many. The emancipation of women, with the concomitant tremendous increase in their sexual freedom, contributed substantially. The decline of parental control over so many young girls has been so great, too, in recent years that one can justifiably say the girl of today enjoys a greater degree of freedom from parental restriction or regulation than did the young man of the same age a few decades ago. It is fashionable nowadays for girls to smoke, to drink, to use make-up lavishly, to stay out at all hours, to avow knowledge of sex and birth-control, to discuss obscene literature and even to take drugs. Much of this vaunted knowledge is erroneous, much more of it is merely bravado; all of it is superficial; many of the paraded sex adventures are apocryphal. Apart from certain fundamentals, it is questionable whether the young woman of today has any more *real* sex knowledge that is of any use to her than had the girl of a previous generation. The difference is that whereas in another age it was the vogue to simulate complete innocence as regards anything remotely connected with sex, nowadays it is the practice to pretend to be thoroughly at home with and inured to all aspects of sex. It is easy, as so many modern ignorant parents do, and as the young themselves do, to mistake precocity for knowledge.

Another factor has been the entry of women, in such overwhelming numbers, into the business world and into the professions, in competition with men. This has led to an increase in the promiscuity of women, a lowered standard of morals generally, and a decrease in the resistance offered to man's erotic advances. In certain cases also the continuance of the girl's position is dependent upon her complacency, in other instances seduction is the price that must be paid to obtain promotion. Every woman is a potential prostitute, just as every man is a potential consorter with prostitutes. It is mainly a question of price, using the word price in a larger and more comprehensive sense than simply a matter of money. The girl who will reject with scorn the proposals of a man belonging to her own station in life will prove easy prey to the social or stage celebrity; the lady of aristocratic birth may succumb gleefully to the advances of a prince.

Before woman's emancipation, as was evident from the inquiry in a preceding chapter into the reasons for women taking to prostitution as a profession, a girl in any but the peasant class had one profession open to her, and one only, that of marriage. Her whole aim in life was to make a good match: in other words, to find a man who would provide her with a home for life. For this reason she prized her virginity as she prized a rare and expensive jewel. And it was this prize which she everlastingly dangled in front of man. Today marriage is no longer the big and important thing it was. True, most normal girls look upon a successful marriage as the culmination of their careers, but they no longer are obsessed with the urgency and the necessity of it. In most cases, they defer any serious contemplation of marriage until they have had that "good time" which nowadays is on every girl's lips. This means that, while matrimony is relegated to the shadowy future, sex adventures loom up more importantly than ever. Virginity is laughed at as something terribly old-fashioned. So much so that those who stress its importance are in danger of being accused of worse practices than normal sexual promiscuity. The modern girl's credo is to drink her fill of enjoyment while she is young or while she can, the future being a nebulous gamble. She puts herself deliberately and repeatedly into environments and circumstances designed to induce and to develop sexual excitement, often in the company of men she hardly knows, and she indulges increasingly in promiscuous intercourse as the inevitable aftermath.

Such causes are responsible for the fact that today, more by far than ever before in the world's history, there are, in every city in Europe and America, large numbers of girls of respectability who are willing, for all sorts of reasons, to meet men halfway in the hunt for sexual excitement and satisfaction. These are the amateur prostitutes of modern civilisation. The net result of this is that the professional prostitute's life is becoming an increasingly difficult one. She has to meet the competition of these amateurs, and inevitably she sees more and more her potential army of clients decreasing. The average man on the hunt for sexual adventure, prefers immensely to obtain what he wants from one of these amateurs than from a professional. He has always preferred the amateur to the professional, the respectable girl to the prostitute. But until recent times it was impossible for more than a fraction of the men of any country to find girls who were not professional harlots whom they could approach with safety. More and further, there could rarely be anything regular in these orgies with girls of respectability.[1] They were, for the most part, fortuitous affairs, to be taken advantage of when opportunity offered, and not in any sense to be looked upon as providing regular means for the indulgence of libidinous desires. And so, in the overwhelming main, men had to rely upon getting their sexual needs satisfied by the professional prostitute.

There are various reasons why, now that the amateur harlot looms so large on the horizon, men prefer her. For one thing she is less expensive. It is rare that any money is asked for or offered. The girl, in nine cases out of ten, would scorn any such idea. The cost of a drink or two, a theatre seat, a box of chocolates, is usually all that the man is called upon to pay. In many cases he pays nothing at all. But the question of cost is not the main reason which leads the man to prefer the

---

[1] For the wealthy, of course, there were the charming private rooms which were once a feature of the principal restaurants of the leading European capitals. In London they existed up to about 1930, some of the finest facilities available being on the top floor of the famous Café Royal in Regent Street before it was rebuilt.

amateur. Another compelling reason which weighs with him is the dread of venereal disease. There is a fallacious idea, widely disseminated and firmly established, that nearly every professional *fille de joie* is afflicted with one of the venereal infections. There is similarly a coincident and equally fallacious idea current that the amateur fornicator, who is not considered to be a prostitute at all, is free from infection. Finally, there is the preference which nearly every man has for a girl who has not been common property of a number of other men.

XVI: THE TRAFFIC IN WOMEN

ONE outcome of latter-day brothel prostitution is what is generally and popularly known as "white-slave" traffic. The term is a misnomer. Not by any means all the girls who are inveigled into becoming brothel prostitutes or mistresses belong to the white races. In the East the brothels are thronged with women of every shade of black and yellow; and these coloured girls are searched for by those engaged in the business of prostitution with the same diligence as are girls with paler skins.

In every country in the world where the number of males is largely in excess of the number of females, either permanently or temporarily, the demand for prostitutes is a considerable one. In newly settled countries and in other spots where, for any reason whatever, women are in the minority, this applies. Thus the demand may shift from one place to another in accordance with the movements of men. This is well exemplified in the case of troops moving from country to country. Wherever there is such movement there is a demand for women. In the case of soldiers the demand is for the cheaper type of prostitute. Then again the erotic requirements of wealthy men, even where the shortage of women is not a particularly noticeable feature, are a factor not to be overlooked. These men are constantly requiring fresh mistresses.

As the charms of one girl wear off, a new mistress is called for. And some men have a strong predilection for virgins. Then again, there are men willing to pay phenomenally high prices for girls or women who are willing to be parties to perverse sexual practices. They prefer, too, in many cases, women of a foreign race. Inevitably there is an added incentive where novelty can be introduced into the basic allurement of sex.

Even where the supply of native women may be adequate, it is often difficult to fill the brothels with girls of a type which the clients of these brothels require. In *all countries* having brothels and a licensing system, with or without medical inspection, it is becoming increasingly difficult to obtain recruits in sufficient numbers from among the native population. The conditions of life in these brothels, the poor remuneration, and other drawbacks, cause girls more and more to engage in free-lance prostitution; and, in countries where free-lance prostitution is not allowed, to elude registration as long as possible. In consequence, in brothels which rely upon recruiting their inmates from the local population they have to be content, in the majority of cases, with the lowest type of harlot. Often these brothels are people with raddled old whores. The only way to secure the services of pretty young girls is for the owners to get foreign girls into their clutches.

There is, too, yet another reason which applies in certain countries where the bulk of the prostitutes are aliens; a reason which not only leads to the retention of a system which encourages the importation of foreign women, but also prevents any measures being taken to deport such women as have entered the country.[1] This reason is simply that the governments of these countries consider the employment of foreign prosti-

---

[1] Deportation of alien women was one of the methods of combating the traffic in women recommended by the League of Nations Investigation Committee.

tutes affords a considerable degree of protection to their own girls and women.

The brothels of the South American republics and Middle East countries are always looking for European women suitable for their purpose. Obviously the continued existence of brothels depends on a steady supply of new women, and this demand induces traffickers to maintain their efforts. A League of Nations Report in 1927 said "It is the existence of licensed houses which supplies the traffickers and their accomplices with a sure and permanent market for their services." Before the war, the League estimated that there were 4,500 foreign prostitutes in Buenos Aires alone, and even now, according to one authority, French girls, exported via Marseilles and Bordeaux, outnumber their Argentinian ladies of vice.[1]

The business is highly organised and gives employment to a number of intermediaries, all of whom have to earn their livings in one way or another out of the girls whom they provide for the enjoyment of the brothel patrons. There are the *souteneurs*,[2] or other agents, who procure the girls in the first instance, and in some cases live on them; there are the *madames*,[3] who manage the brothels into which the girls are placed; and there are the owners, who provide the capital for the establishment of the brothels and for procuring the girls, but who rarely appear on the actual scene of operation.

The amateur prostitute often falls for the bait offered by the experienced *souteneur*. He takes the girl to the theatre, to the cinema, to dance halls and to restaurants, gives her

[1] *Slaves to Sin: The Trade in Women's Flesh*, by Paul Lefontenay, Luxor Press, 1967, 9/6d.

[2] *Souteneur*—a pimp. Also referred to as "bully" or "ponce" (England), "*Zuhalter*" (Germany), "cadet" (America). Not every pimp is a procurer. The term is applied to a very large number of men connected with prostitution, including those who live on the earnings of prostitutes and those who act as procurers for brothels.

[3] A *madame* has usually herself been a prostitute and knows every phase of the profession.

presents, and acts the part of the wealthy man about town. Eventually he suggests a foreign trip, and usually the bait is swallowed. This method is *sometimes* adopted and occasionally proves successful in the case of respectable girls of poor parentage or orphans, who are working in London or some other city far removed from their homes. With girls of these types, if all other plans fail, marriage, bogus or real, overcomes every difficulty.

Chorus girls and artistes attached to low-grade theatres and touring companies, and the hordes of girls of every kind who are anxious to get on the stage, provide a certain number of recruits. It is not difficult for a skilled *souteneur*, posing as a producer or a theatrical agent looking for likely talent for Middle East shows, to induce inexperienced girls to go abroad on these pretences. In many cases the girls are given jobs as dancers, singers or entertainers at cabarets which are really brothels, and sooner or later they are compelled to prostitute themselves. The first step taken, it is not long before they become brothel prostitutes in every sense of the word.

Many of the girls who become "white slaves" do so voluntarily, and even where they may not be exactly aware of the precise nature of their proposed employment, they have a tolerably good idea that promiscuity and immorality are part of the duties expected of them. The bulk of these girls, for one reason or another, are in difficulties. Their difficulties may be of many kinds, though lack of money or prospects of securing employment of a kind they will accept are the predominating motives. Even the actual prostitutes recruited for service in foreign brothels are mainly in distress—the *successful* free-lance prostitute would spit in the face of any trafficker who made overtures to her.

If a young girl can be induced to leave her own country and enter a brothel, she becomes a mere tool in the capable hands of those whose business it is to exploit her. Usually the girl works on a commission basis, but out of this commission she has to pay for clothes, food, perfumes, doctors' fees and graft to the police. In most cases she is constantly in debt to the *madame* who runs the brothel. It is part of the *madame's* policy to see that the girls are indebted to her, as this gives her power over them.

In *Slaves to Sin,* by Paul Lefontenay,[1] the most recent publication on the trade in women's flesh, is a reference to the researches of Karl Barnard, the well-known Swiss sociologist, who has investigated the backgrounds of girls who have become victims of white slavers. Of 500 cases investigated 57 per cent. of girls came from the lower classes, 28 per cent. from the middle classes and 15 per cent. from the upper classes. In the years 1960-65 the total number of women who disappeared in Austria, France, Italy, Germany and Spain, probably to become victims of traffickers, was 5,496. Of these, more than 3,000 came from unhappy, disunited families, and 32 per cent. of them had been in trouble before for running away from home and had been brought back by the police. Of the total, 63 per cent. were between sixteen and twenty-one years of age, and only 7 per cent. were over twenty-five. According to Barnard, the ideal victim of a white-slaver is an adventurous lower-class girl whose parents are divorced, and who can speak no language but her own.

The relations between prostitute and *souteneur* or bully, as he is termed in England, has often proved a puzzle to sociological students. It seems strange that any woman will be willing to prostitute her body in order to keep a man in idleness, who, often enough, is not married to her; especially as it is a well-known fact that these bullies are often cruel to their women. It is held by many that the explanation lies in the fact that the bullies in reality are the lovers of the prostitutes

[1] This fascinating, illustrated, work is published by Luxor Press, London, 9/6d.

who work for them, supplying the psychological factor that is lacking in their clients, and that the attachment of the prostitute to her lover is close and deep. Other observers contend that the true explanation lies in fear. These bullies are cruel, callous criminals who will stop at nothing, and the women who have got into their clutches are afraid to leave them, just as much as they are afraid to give them away to the police. Now I have no doubt both these explanations possess some truth, but they by no means reveal the whole or indeed the main truth. The bully is the woman's protector. Prostitutes are human, like other women. Not all of them are the brazen-faced, hard-mouthed harridans popular opinion personifies; many, even in the lower ranks of the profession, are nothing like a match in hardness, vindictiveness and unscrupulousness for their clients. There are in existence, and in considerable numbers, too, men who do not hesitate to decamp without paying the fee agreed upon. The prostitute cannot invoke the aid of the law in the securing of her just dues. She is socially ostracised, and her word would count for nothing against that of a so-called respectable member of society. It is for these reasons that she often finds a bully, upon whom she can rely to put in an appearance, when called upon, to accord her psychical as well as physical protection, to negotiate on her behalf with landlords, owners of flats, hotel-keepers, and in other business deals, a most valuable aid in the pursuit of her profession. Also there are a number of young, inexperienced and unintelligent prostitutes who not only learn to lean upon some man to look after them, but who would be helpless without guidance. These are the girls who are handed from pimp to pimp, or from brothel to brothel, like so many pieces of merchandise. They are bullied and trampled upon hopelessly. They have no knowledge of their rights as human beings; they have no notion of rebellion.

Mixed up with the traffic in women is the traffic in drugs

and in obscene literature and pictures. Both drugs and obscene publications are sold in brothels at exorbitant prices. Pictures illustrating every form of sexual perversity are part of the stock in trade of many prostitutes.

Most of the girls who are recruited into the trade, even by false pretences, continue to work as prostitutes for some time. They usually do not leave the profession at the first opportunity. The popular idea, fanned by sensational accounts in the Press, in novels and on the films, that these "white slaves" are virtually prisoners and cannot escape, once they are "within the toils," is often nonsense. Even allowing for the difficulties occasioned through being in a foreign country, with the language of which they are unfamiliar, they are not kept inside a prison cell. They might somehow escape if they wanted to, and there is usually a representative of their own country to whom an appeal could be made. The fact that they put up with their lot is significant. And the reason they put up with their lot is, unless I am greatly mistaken, that they can see no other way of earning a living that they care to adopt.

All warnings issued by governments, by moralists, by social workers, and by others, against entering the profession of prostitution have proved unavailing. You cannot put down vice by warning people against it. Every warning against vice is an advertisement for vice, and attempts to suppress the traffic in women by legislative and other remedial measures have proved only partially successful.

XVII: THE LAW AND PROSTITUTION

In all civilised countries, owing to the fact that the prostitute is treated as a social pariah or outcast, she rarely gets justice. Many men and women, who, in regard to most social problems, are reasonable and just in their reactions, the moment they begin to consider the problems connected with prostitution, become unjust, intolerant and vindictive. They would appear to be incapable of viewing the situation without bias. The protection of young men from consorting with prostitutes, and the prevention of young women from becoming prostitutes, so engage their attention and warp their judgment that they applaud and encourage legislation which singles out for punishment and ostracism one party to the contract while allowing the other equally guilty party to go without any form of punishment whatever and with an umblemished reputation. It is because of this attitude that, every year, in Great Britain, in the United States of America, and in other enlightened countries, girls and women are punished by fine or imprisonment for acts which are not or ought not to be, in themselves, criminal or legal offences—for soliciting, for importuning, for following the profession of prostitute.

In Great Britain, as we have seen, the only efforts in the way of regulation were short-lived ones which proved extremely unpopular. In comparatively recent years there have been various attempts to reintroduce some system of regulation, but they have all been defeated by the opposing bodies, mainly, as we have seen, on the ground that any system of licensing prostitutes is a licensing of vice.

According to English law no action of any kind can be taken against a prostitute solely on the ground that she is a prostitute. For any steps to be taken against her she must have committed some other act which, either in itself or coupled with the fact of her being a prostitute, constitutes an offence. Actually the prostitute is penalised to the extent that, although there is no law against her making her living as a professional prostitute, this very fact, in certain circumstances, may make her actions illegal. Thus an act which in any other woman would constitute no infringement of the law, in the case of a prostitute becomes a nuisance and, as such, constitutes a punishable offence. For instance, a girl who works in a shop or factory can loiter about the streets and ogle men to her heart's content: the self-same action on the part of a "common prostitute" is an offence in the eyes of the law. The Metropolitan Police Act, 1839, Section 54 (11), contained a clause (superseded in 1959) which stated that a common prostitute "loitering or being in thoroughfares[1] for the purpose of prostitution to the annoyance of passengers" might be arrested; and a further clause (Section 54 (13)) reading "every person who shall use any threatening, abusive or insulting words or behaviour with the intent to provoke a breach of the peace or whereby a breach of the peace may be occasioned," which has often in the past been the ground for a charge against a prostitute caught in the act of solicitation. Similarly, Section 3 of the Vagrancy Act 1824, has a clause which provides that "every

---

[1] The act of loitering had to be committed on public property. It was not an offence within the meaning of the Act if committed on private premises. It is for this reason that so many prostitutes made their overtures in arcades not public property. This loophole was closed in 1959.

common prostitute wandering in the public streets or public highways or in any place of public resort and behaving in a riotous or indecent manner" may be considered to be an "idle and disorderly person."[1] These are the clauses which were so often invoked in charging prostitutes. Up to 1959 there was no legislation against female soliciting *per se*.

Section 28 of the Town Police Clauses Act, 1847 (also superseded by the 1959 Act), contained a clause which read: "Every common prostitute or night-walker loitering and importuning passengers for the purpose of prostitution in any street to the obstruction, annoyance or danger of the residents or passengers may be arrested by a constable without warrant, and on summary conviction be fined 40s. or imprisoned 14 days."[2] This law applied to urban areas outside London.

In Scotland, in burghs outside Edinburgh and Aberdeen, the street-walker who loiters about or importunes passengers for the purpose of prostitution commits an offence and is liable to a fine of forty shillings, under the Burgh Police (Scotland) Act 1892, Section 381 (22). Such activity in the two cities named, however, for some reason carries a much bigger penalty, a fine of ten pounds or imprisonment for sixty days. Additional penalties, including imprisonment, may be imposed for further offences within seven years, in all burghs.

It is important to note that "annoyance" was a specific

[1] Such a person became liable to a fine not exceeding five pounds or to imprisonment for not more than a month. A further conviction could lead a prostitute to be deemed a "rogue and vagabond," with penalties not exceeding twenty-five pounds or imprisonment for up to three months. Such a person again convicted could become an "incorrigible rogue" and be sent to quarter sessions for sentence up to one year's imprisonment.

[2] There is a measure, passed in 1825, which is still on the statute book, entitled An Act for the Preservation of Peace and Good Order in the Universities of England, in which there is a clause providing for the arrest of "common prostitutes" who are discovered in university precincts and are unable to give a satisfactory explanation for their presence.

ingredient of the offence in England and Wales, but not in Scotland. Very rarely, of course, would men solicited give evidence of "annoyance," and courts were, unfortunately, content to infer it. There is very little doubt that numerous sentences were passed which, on a strict reading of the law, were unsupported by appropriate evidence.

In London, under the Metropolitan Police Act, 1839, the penalty was a fine of forty shillings. Consequently many women pleaded guilty rather than fight the case. The Wolfenden Report, in 1957, commented that "it was widely felt that the present system whereby a prostitute is repeatedly brought before the courts and automatically disposed of on pleading guilty and paying a fine of forty shillings, which she regards as an indirect and not very onerous form of taxation or licence, is making a farce of the criminal law." The Report recommended that the law relating to street offences be reformulated so as to eliminate the requirement to establish annoyance, and that the maximum penalties be increased, and a system of progressively higher penalties be introduced.

It is typical of the official attitude to sexual matters in Britain that the portion of the Wolfenden Report which dealt with homosexuality and recommended the liberalisation of the law in this respect was quite ignored (until legislation was enacted in 1967 as a result of a Private Member's Bill), while that portion which recommended the stiffening of the law relating to prostitution was promptly followed by the passing into law of the Street Offences Act, 1959.

Under this Act "(1) it shall be an offence for a common prostitute to loiter or solicit in a street or public place for the purpose of prostitution; (2) a person guilty of an offence under this section shall be liable, on summary conviction, to a fine not exceeding ten pounds or, for an offence committed after a previous conviction, to a fine not exceeding twenty-five pounds or, for an offence committed after more than one previous conviction, to a fine not exceeding twenty-five pounds or imprisonment for a period not exceeding three months, or both."

The older Acts which dealt with procuration were the various Criminal Law Amendment Acts. The original Act of 1885, for the passing of which W. T. Stead's sensational articles in *The Pall Mall Gazette* were mainly responsible, raised the age of consent from thirteen to sixteen years.[1] The Act was strengthened on several occasions later, and was eventually superseded by the Sexual Offences Act, 1956, as far as England and Wales are concerned. It remains in force in Scotland.

It is an offence, *inter alia*, to procure a female to become, in any part of the world, a common prostitute, or to procure her to leave the United Kingdom to become an inmate of a brothel elsewhere, or to procure her by threats or intimidation, or by false pretences to have unlawful sexual intercourse, or to drug her for that purpose. There are also special provisions relating to mental defectives, and to taking girls out of the possession of their parents or guardians, and to detaining females against their will for the purpose of unlawful sexual intercourse. In general such offences are punishable by two years' imprisonment. A similar punishment is applicable to any person who is the owner or occupier of premises and who induces or suffers a girl under the age of sixteen to be on the premises for the purpose of having unlawful sexual intercourse, except that if the girl is under thirteen, the person may

[1] Until the passing of the Criminal Law Amendment Act of 1885, all sexual offences against girls came under the Offences Against the Person Act of 1875 (38 and 39 Vic., c. 94), whereby to have carnal knowledge of a girl under twelve years was a felony punishable by penal servitude for life (maximum penalty), and to have carnal knowledge of a girl over twelve and under thirteen, with or without her consent was a misdemeanour punishable by two years' imprisonment (maximum penalty).

be given life imprisonment. It is also an offence for any person in charge of a girl under sixteen to encourage her prostitution, or commit sexual intercourse with, or indecent assault upon her.

There are, however, exceedingly few cases of procuration which come to the notice of the police in Britain, mainly because women who become prostitutes do so without any need for "procuration."

The keeping of brothels and the letting of premises for use as brothels are prohibited in this country. Here the law is clear and definite. It is sufficient to be able to prove that various persons of both sexes are allowed to use the premises for the purpose of illicit sexual intercourse. There is no necessity to prove that the women are actually professional prostitutes; there is no need to prove that the owner or tenant makes a profit out of those who frequent the premises. But there must be more than one prostitute concerned. A woman may take any number of men into her house or room for the purpose of sexual intercourse without interference from the law.[1] But if two women conjointly occupy premises of any kind, and under any pretence, in which they carry on the profession of prostitution, these premises become a brothel. At the same time a police officer cannot raid premises suspected of being used for the purposes of a brothel merely through witnessing the disappearance within the doors of a few couples. The premises must be kept under observation for six consecutive nights. And, according to Bishop,[2] there were wily brothel-keepers in London who pursued their calling indefin-

---

[1] A house in which a number of prostitutes have *separate* rooms or apartments, where the owner of the premises does not live in them or have control over the inmates, is not a brothel within the meaning of the Act. A hotel, however, in which rooms were knowingly rented to prostitutes for the purposes of their profession would constitute a brothel.

[2] Cecil Bishop, *Women and Crime*, 1931.

itely and under the very eyes of the police, having several different houses, and never using any one of these on six consecutive nights.

It is under the Sexual Offences Act, 1956, in England and Wales, or the Criminal Law Amendment Act, 1885, in Scotland, that it is an offence for any person to keep a brothel, or to manage, or act or assist in the management of a brothel. Likewise it is an offence for the lessor or landlord of any premises or his agent to let the whole or part of the premises with the knowledge that they are to be used, in whole or in part, as a brothel, or, where the whole or part of the premises is used as a brothel, to be wilfully a party to that use continuing. Further, it is an offence for the tenant or occupier of any premises knowingly to permit the whole or part of the premises to be used as a brothel or for the purposes of habitual prostitution. The punishment in each instance is a fine of one hundred pounds or imprisonment for three months, or both. On a second or subsequent conviction it is a fine of £250 or imprisonment for six months, or both. In England and Wales, if a tenant has been convicted, the landlord may, subject to certain provisions, determine the lease, and if he fails to do so, could be deemed to be a party to any subsequent offence committed in respect of the premises. In Scotland, a conviction of the tenant automatically voids the lease or arrangement to let.

There are, of course, various aspects of and loopholes in the law which are examined in detail in the Wolfenden Report, which says, however: "As long as society tolerates the prostitute, it must permit her to carry on her business somewhere."

The Licensing Act, 1953, contains a prohibitory clause against a licensee allowing his premises "to be a brothel." There is a maximum penalty of twenty pounds, but he automatically forfeits his licence on conviction. The same Act, which applies in England and Wales, makes the licensee liable to a fine of ten pounds, or, for a subsequent offence, twenty pounds, if he allows his premises to be the habitual resort of reputed prostitutes. This does not mean that a prostitute must not be allowed to enter a public-house, but she must remain on the premises only to obtain such reasonable refreshment as is necessary on the occasion.

In unlicensed refreshment houses there are somewhat similar provisions under the Refreshment Houses Act, 1860, and in Scotland there are prohibitions against the assembly of persons of "notoriously bad fame."

The profession of pimp, or living upon the earnings of a prostitute, is dealt with in England and Wales under the Sexual Offences Act, 1956, which provides that "It is an offence for a man knowingly to live wholly or in part on the earnings of prostitution. For the purposes of this section a man who lives with or is habitually in the company of a prostitute, or who exercises control, direction or influence over a prostitute's movements in a way which shows he is aiding, abetting or compelling her prostitution with others, shall be presumed to be knowingly living on the earnings of prostitution, unless he proves to the contrary." In Scotland there are similar provisions in the Immoral Traffic (Scotland) Act, 1902, and the Criminal Law Amendment Act, 1912.

There are various miscellaneous provisions relating to prostitution in other laws on the statute book, but the principal matters have been outlined above.

Turning to the United States, we find that prostitution is dealt with by the Federal Law; and, in addition, each State has its own supplementary law or laws. Prosecutions are generally made under the Vagrancy Acts, involving the taking of fingerprints, compulsory medical examination and imprisonment in either a workhouse or a reformatory. As fornication itself is a criminal offence according to American law, in many States the mere fact of a man and woman who are unmarried having intercourse may lead to the woman being proceeded against and classed as a prostitute.

The outstanding feature of almost all legislation concerned directly or indirectly with prostitution is that the law is concerned with penalising, where there is any such intent, or regulating, the woman's part. Although prostitution is essentially a dual affair, the law rarely takes any cognisance whatever of the man's share in the act.[1] Nor does it, in Great Britain, take any cognisance of fornication so long as the woman does not make of it a profession.

[1] In some American States, in certain circumstances the male partner can be proceeded against; and, in accordance with the provisions of the Mann Act, the transportation of a woman into another State for the purpose of fornication is a punishable offence.

In the U.S.S.R., when the campaign against prostitution was begun, an important part of it was the publication of the names and addresses of the clients of prostitutes.

XVIII: THE FUTURE OF PROSTITUTION

THE outstanding point resulting from any study of prostitution as it stands today is that professional prostitution is declining. There are fewer prostitutes in London, New York, Paris or any other large city than at most times during the past fifty years. There are fewer prostitutes in brothels, and there are fewer registered prostitutes outside the brothels.

It is contended by some that it is only a question of time before the professional harlot disappears. This, as I shall show, is an attitude which cannot be fully justified. It is quite true that for various reasons, including repressive measures in certain important countries, prostitution is less seen. Even before the Street Offences Act of 1959, however, the London prostitute was much more respectable than was her prototype of fifty years previously. She had been quick to accommodate herself to the changed conditions of the age. She was quieter and better dressed, she spoke better, she was rarely seen drunk on the streets; she was much more circumspect in her behaviour generally; she solicited, true enough, but she employed tact. In short, there were fewer appropriate prosecutions for annoyance and indecent behaviour, because only on rare occasions was there the one or the other. Coincidentally, what is called, by way of contrast, the respectable girl had become more meretricious in her dress, appearance and behaviour. The two, respectable woman and prostitute, more and more tended to meet on common ground. The old-type prostitute who danced about, gaudily and drunkenly, in the Strand, Leicester Square, Piccadilly and Regent Street had become a thing of the past.

All of this does not mean that the world has become more moral; that single men are becoming chaste; that married men are content with their wives. On the contrary, there has been a huge increase in promiscuity among men and an even greater increase among women. It is this increase in promiscuity among women, and the marked decline in moral scruples, that have struck such a severe blow against the profession of prostitution. We have considered all this in some detail in Chapter XV, and the results are that more and more every year man is turning to so-called "respectable girls" in order to satisfy his sexual appetite, and less and less having recourse to professional fornicators.

The decrease, therefore, in professional prostitution is coincident with the extension of promiscuity between so-called people of respectability. Unmistakably the general movement is towards the conditions prevailing in savage and semi-civilised states of society, where there was no specific body of women, either set aside by the government or self-immolated through general ostracism, for the use of men. More and more is there a tendency towards promiscuity—not promiscuity between males and inferior women, whether professional or amateur, but between men and women of the same or equivalent social standing.

Virginity among women is becoming something for the sophisticated to sneer at. This may be deplorable, but it is true. Birth control, if it has done nothing else, has made possible the competition of the amateur fornicator. And now that "the Pill" has been pronounced safe it will no doubt be used by countless women and girls to allow them to fornicate freely without any fear of unwanted pregnancy—though not, of course, without fear of venereal disease.

It is easy to see how any increase in the promiscuity of women generally must have deadly effects on professional prostitution. Apart from the preference of most men for girls outside the ranks of harlotry, to which reference has been made in an earlier chapter, the matter is largely one of economics. It is often cheaper for a man to engage in sexual adventure with respectable girls than with professional harlots.

Coincidentally with this competition from single girls in search of what is loosely termed "a good time," there has, in the past decades, been a phenomenal increase in adultery. It is axiomatic that from the beginning of time adultery has been prostitution's greatest competitor. The rise of one has always been coincident with the decline of the other. Adultery has many advantages for the man. It is, with some sensational exceptions, much less costly; it is infinitely safer; it has charms which are unknown to the consorter with prostitutes. And, in certain circumstances, and in certain circles, it may become fashionable. It has become fashionable in both England and America during recent years.

All these factors are affecting the prostitute's profession simultaneously, and, in consequence, prostitution itself appears to be in a state of transition. It is still, in its more open, more brazen and more meretricious professional forms, something to be sneered at, to be rebuked and to be assailed with moral strictures and indignation: in its veiled, euphemised and surreptitious amateur forms it is something to be overlooked and often enough encouraged.

The temporary respectability of promiscuity is nothing new in itself. We saw an excellent instance of this in the manner in which, during the two world wars, in the blessed name of gratitude, many girls of respectability, and even of gentle

birth, gave themselves to the soldiers without scruple, diffi-
dence or stint.

Together and cumulatively, these new sociological conditions are reducing the number of professional prostitutes. In
the ordinary course of events it would appear that the downward course will continue. There is no likelihood that the
factors which are inducing this decrease will fall off in their
effects or diminish in extent; quite the contrary, there is every
likelihood that they will increase in scope and effect, and that
there will be an extension of other disruptive factors which as
yet are in their infancy. For instance, promiscuity in women
is likely to increase, not only as a result of the latter-day freedom, but also through the disinclination of men to marry at
an early age; the changed outlook on adultery, which verges
upon its being approved by society; and the vanishing of the
social ostracism which for so many centuries has been associated with pre-marital sexual intercourse. In addition, there is
the extension of both male and female homosexuality and
perverse sexual practices, which to a certain limited extent
are displacing prostitution.

It is a consideration of all these several factors that has
led to the notion that professional prostitution may disappear
in civilised States. It is true, as I have attempted to prove,
that where all are practising what is virtually prostitution
there can be no such thing as prostitution. Thus any considerable extension of the existing flagrant promiscuity among
women of respectability would inevitably reduce prostitution
to relatively small dimensions. But even so, it would not
cause prostitution to disappear completely. And the reasons for
this call for no very diligent search.

The promiscuity of the modern girl is a selective promiscuity. It cannot be denied that men are finding more and
more that they can get for nothing what in previous generations had to be paid for. But this does not apply to *all men.*

In by far the great majority of cases, any such gratuitous sexual favours are restricted to young men. They are certainly not likely, for instance, to be granted to the physically handicapped, who also have sexual needs.

It is a well-known fact that the clients of prostitutes, in the great majority, are married men. They are married men who, for a number of reasons, find it necessary or desirable to seek sexual solace at the hands of women other than their wives. I have already, in the first section of this work, referred to the fact that a woman's sexual anaesthesia is often directly responsible for driving her husband to seek some other outlet for his erotic passion. A very large number of wives are inconsiderate. The inconsiderateness and selfishness of man where his sexual appetite is concerned are made much of in books and sex guides, but both are at least equalled, and very often they are excelled, by the sexual inconsiderateness and selfishness of woman. Most married women of all but the very poorest classes take the attitude that intercourse is something to be indulged in according to their own appetites and inclinations—they overlook or they ignore the fact that, owing to man's different physiological make-up, in actual fact the man is often the party who should decide this point. All these sexual disharmonies are disturbing and dissatisfying; their cumulative effect is the breeding of indifference. The man, somewhat naturally, turns to a woman upon whom he can depend to satisfy his appetite at the time of its existence. He turns to the prostitute. There are, too, the monthly periods when any woman resents intercourse; then there are long stretches when the pregnant woman cannot, with safety, indulge in the sexual act; there are times of illness. Some men, true enough, religiously practise abstention during any and all such times. But this by no means applies to all. The majority either cannot or will not be abstemious; they prefer to patronise prostitutes.

Because of the hypocritical attitude towards sex which is so manifest, even today, in Britain and America, coupled with the lack of adequate sex education, many marriages are doomed to prove failures. This does not mean they necessarily end in divorce; it means something much worse, it means the continuance of the union in circumstances where both partners are unhappy and frustrated. In many cases the wife, for any one of several reasons basically resultant from ignorance of sex, is indifferent or looks upon her marital duties with repulsion. Inevitably, sooner or later, the husband is driven to consort with other women. In other cases the failure of the husband to cultivate the art of love is responsible for the marriage degenerating into a partnership which merely continues to exist by mutual toleration.

In addition, there are those men, married and single, young and old, who are sexual perverts and desire the gratification of their appetites by perverse practices. They are incapable of having coitus in any normal fashion, or of being sexually excited in the ordinary way. Fetishists, sadists, and masochists —there are many such. Their wives, their mistresses, their girl friends, cannot or will not satisfy their desires. For one thing, they have not the requisite knowledge, these girls of respectability and of orthodox morality. For another thing, they would reject with scorn and indignation any instructions or proposals connected with such practices. In such cases, therefore, resort is made to prostitutes.

It is extremely unlikely that women of respectability will ever compete with the professional prostitute in this matter of satisfying the sexual requirements of male perverts, senescents and satyrs. For this reason alone prostitution in some form will survive. For this reason alone it will remain a social problem so long as civilisation exists.

Any hope held by persons imbued with ethical and reformative principles of abolishing professional prostitution by the persecution of its practitioners is futile. Freed, in his admirable study of prostitution in Johannesburg, gives striking evidence of the failure of punitive steps in the war on prostitution. He states: "The legal statutes in regard to prostitution in the Province of the Transvaal leave no aspect of the problem untouched. Soliciting, brothel-keeping, procuration, living on the earnings of a prostitute, etc., are all severely dealt with by the law."[1] He goes on to say: "Nevertheless, the penal measures operated by the law in respect of both adult and juvenile prostitution have not reduced the volume of prostitution in the progress of time, nor have they, in the majority of instances, served as a deterrent to prostitutes with previous convictions."[2] His opinion is strikingly confirmed by the Wolfenden Report, which states: "Prostitution is a social fact deplorable in the eyes of moralists, sociologists and, we believe, the great majority of ordinary people. But it has persisted in many civilisations throughout many centuries, and the failure of attempts to stamp it out by repressive legislation shows that it cannot be eradicated through the agency of the criminal law."[3] These facts are brimming with a significance that cannot be overlooked or disregarded.

The history of prostitution, as unfolded in the foregoing pages, presents one outstanding lesson. This lesson is that the most that can be expected from punitive and repressive measures, social ostracism and moral injunction, is the driving of prostitution into underground channels. Only an alteration in economic conditions of so profound and revolutionary a character and conception as to verge on Utopianism,

[1] Louis Franklin Freed, *The Problem of European Prostitution in Johannesburg*, Juta & Co., Cape Town and Johannesburg, 1949, p. 372.
[2] *Ibid.*
[3] Report of the Committee on Homosexual Offences and Prostitution, London, H.M.S.O., 1957.

could, even in these days of widespread selective promiscuity, reduce the number of professional women to the lowest limits possible in a society where men retain their virility, and where it is possible to keep the demand for the services of professional women within the above-defined circumscribed limits.

INDEX